Health

Health Sciences Library
Education Centre
Ashford & St. Peter's Hospitals NHS Trust
London Road
Ashford, Middlesex TW15 3AA

HEALTH

Second edition

Mildred Blaxter

polity

Copyright © Mildred Blaxter 2010

The right of Mildred Blaxter to be identified as Author of this Work has been asserted in accordance with the UK Copyright, Designs and Patents Act 1988.

First edition published in 2004
Second published in 2010 by Polity Press

Polity Press
65 Bridge Street
Cambridge CB2 1UR, UK

Polity Press
350 Main Street
Malden, MA 02148, USA

All rights reserved. Except for the quotation of short passages for the purpose of criticism and review, no part of this publication may be reproduced, stored in a retrieval system, or transmitted, in any form or by any means, electronic, mechanical, photocopying, recording or otherwise, without the prior permission of the publisher.

ISBN-13: 978-0-7456-4845-3
ISBN-13: 978-0-7456-4846-0(pb)

A catalogue record for this book is available from the British Library.

Typeset in 10.5 on 12 pt Sabon
by SNP Best-set Typesetter Ltd., Hong Kong
Printed and bound in Great Britain by MPG Books Group Ltd, Bodmin, Cornwall

The publisher has used its best endeavours to ensure that the URLs for external websites referred to in this book are correct and active at the time of going to press. However, the publisher has no responsibility for the websites and can make no guarantee that a site will remain live or that the content is or will remain appropriate.

Every effort has been made to trace all copyright holders, but if any have been inadvertently overlooked the publisher will be pleased to include any necessary credits in any subsequent reprint or edition.

For further information on Polity, visit our website: www.politybooks.com

Contents

Acknowledgement

This book was originally derived from a series of lectures presented to students in their first year of the Medical School in the University of East Anglia. Thanks are due to Professor Sam Leinster, Inaugural Dean of the Medical School, for his enterprising and generous belief that a sociological view of the concept of 'health' was one of the first things that prospective doctors should be introduced to.

Introduction

I don't think I know when I am healthy, I only know if I am ill. (Office worker aged twenty-eight, UK, Blaxter 1990)

Health is both your inner and your outer state – the state of your soul – being more optimistic, not giving in to any kind of difficulties, trying to find some kind of compromise . . . and also, probably, being needed by society too, however old you are. (Nurse aged fifty two, Moscow, Manning and Tikhonova 2009)

I think that if one day I wake up and I'm seventy, and I've lived like that, then I will say that's good health . . . in short, it will have been life without incident. (Woman, France, Herzlich 1973)

Health is a state of mind, about knowing what to do and how to do it, how to cope. (Male clerical worker aged fifty-four, UK, Blaxter 2004)

My health is a reflection of my lifestyle – I need to be spiritually, mentally, emotionally and physically whole to be truly healthy. I believe complete wholeness is only attainable through reconciliation with God. (Herbalist, UK, Stainton Rogers 1991)

What is health? That's a silly question! (Driver aged thirty-nine, UK, Blaxter 1990)

What is health? Many studies have asked ordinary people this question, and their replies, as these brief examples from research in different countries show, range from the thought ful to the dismissive. Few people think about their health all of the time, but for most it is, at least intermittently, an important topic. How are you? The common greeting may not actually expect an answer in medical terms, but health is one of the most ubiquitous topics of conversation in everyday life. At the same time, health and medicine are major sections of the social organization of any society, and a great deal of resources and manpower go into systems for the promotion of health and the management of disease.

It may seem obvious that we must know what 'health' is. However, it is not only something on which individuals can have very different views, but also a concept which has inspired endless theorizing and dispute throughout the centuries.

This volume attempts to summarize where we are now, in the early twenty-first century, in thinking about health. The emphasis is on contemporary ideas and their development during the last century or so. A historical approach is the starting point, and consideration of the latest developments and speculation about how the concept of health is changing is a major focus. The emphasis is upon what is known as 'Western scientific medicine', because this is the system to which most developed societies subscribe and which tends to be adopted by most developing societies. This is not, though, to denigrate other, non-Western, systems of belief, or to ignore the way in which 'alternative' ideas are incorporated into modern ideas of health.

The central discipline here is medical sociology. But others make contributions – psychology, biological science, clinical medicine, social epidemiology, philosophy, anthropology, history of medicine, policy and politics. This, again, shows how deeply embedded ideas about health are, and how many perspectives may be brought to bear.

The volume is not presented as a textbook of the whole of medical sociology, or a review of all the facts and figures of what is usually called social medicine. Rather than a text-book, it is an introduction to *ideas* about health, which may provide students of any of these disciplines, and especially those in medicine, nursing, and other health professions, with provocative ways of thinking about its social aspects. It attempts to demonstrate the particular contribution of modern social science to medicine, and, while keeping references to research studies to a minimum, it introduces some of the best writing and all the most important scholars on the subject. Since concepts are not easily reduced to statistics, most of the material is qualitative rather than quantitative. The topic is, as far as possible, health rather than illness, and health rather than health-care systems.

This revised edition not only brings the text up to date, but introduces new material which relates especially to current developments in science and technology which are fundamentally altering our perceptions of the body and redefining health.

Besides its intellectual interest, the book has practical relevance for health systems and those who study or work in the health-care professions. As will become evident, ways of defining health have always influenced the practice of healers and the organization of care, and continue to play a part in determining the social policies of nations. The meaning of health is neither simple nor unchanging.

1

How is Health Defined?

Health may be defined differently by doctors and their patients, and over time and place. One of the most pervasive definitions, though, is simply normality, with illness as a deviation from the normal. The definition of disease as abnormality or damage – physiological, biochemical or psychological – held sway in modern thought for most of the last century. It is represented in lay thought by the replies commonly given in surveys to an invitation to define health: health is not being ill, health is having no disease. It is represented in clinical medicine by the whole array of tests and standards, rapidly growing in sophistication, to measure 'normal' body size and weight, blood composition, lung capacity, functioning of the liver, and so on, through every organ and system of the body.

This definition raises many problems, however. What is normal – normal for what, and for whom? (Clinical standards usually assume for a particular age and gender, but no more.) 'Normal' can have many meanings: average, most representative, the most common value, central in a distribution, the habitual or the best. Are we talking about the average for a given population, or some ideal? The 'perfect' is not only impossible of attainment, but also not necessarily to be desired. As Hippocrates noted in the *Aphorism*s:

> In athletics a perfect condition that is at its highest pitch is treacherous. Such conditions cannot stay the same or remain

at rest, and, change for the better being impossible, the only possible change is for the worse.

On the other hand, normal defined as average may not mean perfectly healthy, and the average – consider the examples of body weight or cholesterol level – may not be at all what clinicians regard as the 'norm' or ideal to be aimed for. What is normal degeneration in old age: are all the old unhealthy? Not all deviations from the normal are to be deplored or 'treated': some can be positively beneficial, and others are irrelevant to health. Erde (1979: 36) noted:

> If you are 80 or running a marathon, what is normal would differ from the 'norm' of someone age 20 or asleep. Furthermore, if you can run two marathons and no one else can, you may be abnormal and yet as healthy as can be. If your IQ is 100 it is normal. If it is 140, your mind's functions are not in a normal state. We need to know what 'normal' means, before we can tell whether someone has it or is it.

In other words, normal can be descriptive or proscriptive, and if it is proscriptive it has to depend on the state of knowledge at the time, or accepted current theory. A softer version is the recognition that there is a great range of normal variability, and only that which falls outside it need be considered as ill health. The range has still to be defined, perhaps arbitrarily.

Health as the absence of illness

For a time in the mid-twentieth century there was promulgation of the idea of disease or ill health as those phenomena which deviate from the norm in such a way as to place the individual at biological disadvantage. The healthy are those who are not biologically disadvantaged. To some extent this avoids the problems of the definition of normality, since those deviations which have no consequences are irrelevant. But it created new problems in the definition of disadvantage, which was usually described very specifically as shortened life and reduced fertility.

Commentators in the field of mental health used this to argue opposed positions: though no physiological abnormalities had so far been found to account for a condition such as schizophrenia, nevertheless it was a disease, using the biological disadvantage criteria. On the other hand, it was pointed out that many forms of mental ill health did not reduce life expectancy or fertility: was it impossible to call them diseases? In general, the focus on length of life and fertility seemed too Darwinian (disease is anything which interferes with the preservation of the species) and too restrictive.

A more subjective view can be taken, of course, resting the definition of health not on measurable, clinically defined abnormality, but on people's own perception of the experience of symptoms or feelings of illness. The problem is that the norm becomes even more difficult to define. It is commonly demonstrated in studies of populations that to experience no symptoms of ill health at all – never to have pain, mild dysfunction, infection or injury – is in fact highly abnormal: most of us, most of the time, can identify something which we might call a symptom of an illness. Only a small proportion of this is taken for professional attention and diagnosis as disease, and much of it is self-limiting.

Any definition of health as the absence of self-perceived illness has to deal with the fact that this perception varies widely among individuals and depends on situations. Questions have again to be raised about normal illness – normal for this particular person, normal for this sort of individual, normal in these circumstances? – with even less certainty about what the average is, or what would be considered as the ideal.

Disease as deviance

The idea of health as the absence of disease or illness, and disease as deviation from the norm, elides easily into ill health seen as 'deviance' from social or moral norms. The objective observation of a lack of 'normality' meets a very ancient and universal tendency to see the sick person as in some way morally tainted or bewitched. Possibly, they are responsible for their own condition, and at best they are being offered the opportunity to gain merit or show their strength of character in enduring suffering. Ill health usually has negative connotations, and is spoken of as 'bad luck' for the individual. Ill health also harms the functioning or the prosperity of society: the sick are not productive, they may require resources, and they must be controlled and monitored. Thus the American sociologist Talcott Parsons's treatment of sickness as a role designed to allow 'deviants' to find conditional and provisional legitimacy was influential in early medical sociology.

Health as balance or homeostasis

A link between the concepts of health and normality lies in the ancient idea of homeostasis – the idea that the normal state of the body is order, and its systems are designed to be self-righting. This old idea was given new life when it was realized that not only a pathogen, but also a host – the body which was being invaded or harmed – was actively involved in the development of ill health. When a system was being attacked by a specific agent, or was disordered by biological error or stresses and accidents in the environment, regulatory mechanisms came into play. Restoring the normal involves not only equilibrium of the human organism – mind and body – with its environment, but also internal equilibrium within the body's functions and organs. Ill health arises when the balance is disturbed. In modern times this approach gained attraction from its association with the growth of ecology as a natural science.

As commentators such as Mishler (1981) have pointed out, this has elements of older, perhaps less scientific concepts. It echoes the classical Platonic model of health as harmony among the body's processes and systems, with disease as a state of discord, and the Galenian concept of disease as a disturbance of function. Before the rise of modern medicine, not only the cultures of the West but all the great cultures of the world, such as those of China or India, held that health is to be defined as the right balance between supernatural beings, the environment, and processes within the body. Disease as imbalance had to be corrected by the remedying of deficiency (by, for instance, diet) or the removal of excess (by, for instance, purging or bleeding).

A theory of health has to accommodate the fact that all living things have some ability to respond to changing environments. The commonly accepted stance is that the environment does not wholly determine the properties of the organism which is, at least partly, self-organized and capable of change. Modern medicine shows that in certain physiological aspects the body is indeed a homeostatic machine: for instance, the immune system responds when infection enters the system, and loss of blood by injury is responded to by vasoconstriction to keep blood pressure steady. The capacity to sustain equilibrium, or more generally the ability of the body to heal itself, can be regarded as a measure of its healthiness. These ideas, ancient in principle, are elaborated by the findings of modern science. As a total model of health, however, homeostasis has limitations. This is undoubtedly part of healthiness, but some healthy functions – reproduction, for instance – upset equilibrium rather than maintain it, and not all systems are even theoretically self-righting. It can be accepted that some aspects of equilibrium are crucial to life, without confusing the idea of homeostasis with the broader ideal of the normal.

Health as function

This does, however, move away a little from the essentially negative definitions. Another, and even more positive, way is in terms of function. Health is being able to do things. This can be a very basic definition: as a woman of 70 said, when asked what it means to be healthy,

Health is being able to walk around better and doing some work in the house when my knees let me. (Blaxter 1990)

Functional health can be thought of in terms of having a fit body, not being restricted in any way, being able to do the things one wants or needs to do, all the natural functions of ordinary life being performed freely and without pain. This, again, connects to modern ecological ideas by being defined as being well adapted to the environment, engaging in effective interaction with the physical and social world. Ill health is incapacity, whether caused by disease, accident, the degeneration of old age, or less than perfectly functional development at the start of life. Disease is failure in adaptation, and is dysfunctional both to individuals themselves and to the societies of which they are a part.

Another popular functional definition of health is as 'the ability to reach desired goals' (Porn 1993), essentially a concept in terms of adaptive functioning. There are some obvious problems with this definition of health. As Levy (2007) noted, a natural baseline is difficult to define, for people – even in the same place and time – can vary biologically because of a myriad of influences, and normal expectations for one individual can be highly abnormal for another. It depends on what one wants or needs to do: perfect function in a young athlete and in an elderly, sedentary person represents different physical capacities. And functional incapacity is not necessarily dependent on health – as Erde (1979: 35) commented: 'Being stuck in a door would automatically make someone unhealthy if this definition were held.'

Health as function easily progesses into health as fitness, with the question 'fitness for what?' unanswered. A very restricted answer is simply 'the activities of daily living' – mobility, caring for oneself, working. This immediately tends to define those with physical, sensory or mental disabilities as unfit and raises questions about whether impairments – inability to see or hear, for instance – are to be called ill health. Those who speak for people with disabilities would contest this fiercely, arguing that any impairment is more or less disabling depending on the environment: there are disabling environments, not disabled people.

Health as state or status

Confusion commonly arises because of another problem: is health to be defined as a temporary state (am I ill today?) or a longer-term status (am I basically a healthy or unhealthy person?)? That people themselves clearly make this distinction is attested to by replies to polite questions such as 'How are you?', which are often 'Well, I have a cold, but in general I'm very healthy', or answers in health surveys to questions such as 'Are you in good/fair/poor health?', which can take difficult-to-categorize forms such as 'I've got diabetes, but my health is excellent.'

The distinction is not entirely the one which medicine conventionally adopts between the acute and the chronic. All ill health cannot be forced into one of these two categories: people may be 'chronic' sufferers from acute conditions, long-term chronic disease results in varying degrees of acute illness at any particular time. 'State' represents the present health state of the individual, distinct from (though of course commonly associated with) their health status or the general characteristic of being healthy or unhealthy. Health 'status' is a longer term attribute, changing rapidly only in the event of the sudden and unexpected onset of serious illness or permanently damaging trauma. Health state, on the other hand, is an erratic condition, relevant to health status only if it derives from it or if (because of its typicality or frequency) it reflects back to be incorporated into health status.

Health state and health status have some association with the health economist's concept of health as 'stock' or capital and health as 'flow'. Health capital (see p. 25) can be conceived of as the cumulation of health states – illnesses, accidents, malfunctions, increases or decreases in fitness – which the individual or the group experiences.

The biomedical model

There are thus many ways in which health might be defined, for the most part resting on ideas of the 'normal' and of seeing health as opposed to disease or illness. In practice, the definition of health has always been formally the territory of those who define its opposite: healers, or practitioners of medicine as a science or a body of practical knowledge. Since medicine is one of society's major systems, it is obvious that it is these definitions which will be institutionalized and embodied in law and administration, though the extent to which 'lay' models add to or diverge from this body of ideas will be considered later.

The basic paradigm of medicine since the development of the germ theory in the nineteenth century has been what is called the biomedical model. In its stereotypical form, this has been based on, and almost wholly dominated by, the methods and principles of the biological sciences. Such a model would naturally be based on the 'disease' which it is the function of medicine to treat, and thus on ill health rather than health.

Historians of medicine note how two ways of thinking about health have appeared and disappeared throughout the development of Western medical practice. Disease can be seen as independent of the patient:

> The doctor will be different in the Western tradition, because he will be looking through the ill person to the disease that caused the illness. The trained doctor will have a form of contract, not with individuals, but with the diseases that use these individuals as media. (Neve 1995: 479)

Alternatively, as in Hippocratic medicine, the individual, with all his or her particular circumstances, diet, dreams and habits, can be seen as of first importance.

The first way came to predominate after the Enlightenment, when the work of scientists such as Pasteur and Koch in the nineteenth century demonstrated that specific diseases could be introduced into the body by specific microorganisms. The earlier 'anatomists' and pathologists had begun to trace out the structures of the body and the way it functioned, introducing mechanistic models of the processes involved. The new bacteriological science now, however, transformed notions of the practice of medicine. It meant that doctors need no longer be limited by their observation of mechanical processes or rely on accounts of subjective symptoms. Science, and the body's own immune system, could conquer ancient scourges such as cholera, diphtheria or tuberculosis by vaccination and inoculation.

The fundamental principles of the biomedical model began to include the following;

(1)   The first principle is what is called the doctrine of specific etiology, that is, the idea that all disease is caused by theoretically identifiable agents such as germs, bacteria or parasites. The influence of germ theory was powerful, spreading rapidly from infectious diseases to others produced by known, specific, causes – metabolic processes, disturbances of growth or function. An obvious corollary of such a model is that explanation will be thought to be 'better' – more complete – the more that description has moved from an initial taxonomy, or categorization, of individual symptoms through the identification of a 'syndrome' or cluster of symptoms to a final diagnosis of a disease with a single cause.

Criticisms of this principle focused principally on the suggestion that it oversimplified biological processes now known to be very complex. For many diseases there are multiple and interacting causes. Moreover, such a principle looks only to the agent of disease, and ignores the host, and the possibilities of biological adaptation. The scientist and medical historian Rene Dubos, in his influential books *Mirage of Health* and *Man Adapting* nearly half a century ago, asked, for instance, why does infection not always produce disease? Why is disease comparatively rare though infectious agents are present everywhere? The principle is much more easily applicable to acute conditions than to chronic ill health and is difficult to apply to mental disorders.

(2)   A second principle of the biomedical model is called the assumption of generic disease – the idea that each disease has its own distinguishing features that are universal, at least within the human species. These will be the same in different cultures and at different times, unless the disease-producing agent itself changes. As Sydenham declared in the seventeenth century: 'All diseases should be reduced to certain definite

species with the same care which we see exhibited by botanists in their description of plants.'

Criticisms of this focus on the rather obvious point that diseases are differently defined in different cultures and that medical definitions of disease have clearly changed over time. Each new advance in knowledge of physiology and each new wave of technology has added new definitions of ill health to the accepted canon. Despite the doctrine of specific etiology, many conditions which are still only symptoms or syndromes are recognized within medicine as 'diseases'. More generally, it can easily be shown (chapter 2) that what is viewed as illness in any particular society and at any historical time depends on cultural norms and social values.

It has been argued that in practice a condition is defined by medicine as a disease if and when it is felt that clinical means are appropriate for treating it: ill health is simply what doctors treat. The answer that doctors give to the question 'Is this a disease?' is really an answer to the question 'Can I, or do I want to, treat this person?' (Linder 1965). This is not always true, of course, for doctors treat many people they do not see as 'diseased'. But it can be demonstrated that frequently the act of diagnosis is primarily the process of deciding what the appropriate treatment is (Blaxter 1978).

Thus 'new' diagnoses – new diseases – such as alcoholism, post-traumatic stress disorder, chronic fatigue syndrome, are born through an interaction of new knowledge about both their possible causes and how they might possibly be helped. As a definition of disease, 'what doctors treat' has obvious problems, however. It implies that no one can be ill until recognized as such, and leaves the concept at the mercy of idiosyncratic individual medical decisions.

(3) A third principle of scientific biomedicine is that it accepts the model of all ill health as deviation from the normal, especially the normal range of measurable biological variables. In the mid-nineteenth century Virchow proclaimed that disease was simply altered physiology: 'Nothing but life under altered conditions.' There is an association with the definition of health as equilibrium and disease as a disturbance of the body's functions, with the purpose of medical technology the restoration to equilibrium. The immune, or

endocrine, or neuropsychological, systems attempt to restore the 'normal', and the purpose of medicine is to instigate or assist this process. But medical science now realizes that the human organism has no set pattern for structure and function, and it is often unclear where normal variation ends and abnormality begins. Kendall (1975: 305) asked: 'Is hypertension a disease, and if so what is the level beyond which the blood pressure is abnormal?', and suggested that it was in fact this example of hypertension which finally discredited the nineteenth-century assumption that there was always an observable, measurable distinction between illness and normal health.

(4)   The fourth postulate of medical science was that it was held to be based on the principles of scientific neutrality. Medicine adopts not only the rational method of science but also its values – objectivity and neutrality on the part of the observer, and the view of the human organism as simply the product of biological (and perhaps psychological) processes over which the individuals themselves have little control.

The reply to this is that the practice of medicine, whatever its theory, is always deeply embedded in the larger society. It cannot be neutral, for there are wider social, political and cultural forces dictating how it does its work and how the unhealthy are dealt with. The diagnoses of female hysteria in the nineteenth century, or Gulf War Syndrome in the twenty-first, cannot be thought to be culturally or politically neutral.

Contemporary biomedicine

Residues of all four of these postulates can be found in contemporary medical practice. But it would be a caricature to present them as defining modern medicine: it is a long time since the medical model espoused crude models of cause and effect. The assumption that every disease had a distinct cause, which was both necessary and sufficient, had to be given up as it became apparent that a great many interacting factors, whether inside or outside the individual body, contributed to any ill health. To regard one as the cause became increasingly arbitrary. During the first half of the twentieth century, for instance, it was noted that the tubercular baccillus was a necessary cause of tuberculosis – that is, the disease would not be present if the agent was absent – but it was not a sufficient cause. The baccillus was widespread in many populations, but only a minority of people actually developed the disease.

The model of the causation of ill health changed from the simple, direct effect of a bacillus or virus, to include the immune system as intermediary, and eventually to include a wide range of influences on the agent and on the host's response to it.

Biomedicine now admits multiple and interactive causes, and that the whole may be more than simply the sum of the parts. The rise of psychology was also relevant in altering the purely mechanistic model of illness. Increasingly evidence was gathered – to add sufficient scientific proof to what had probably always been personally felt and professionally recognized – to show that psychological factors affect many illness conditions, and many if not most conditions have some psychosomatic elements: that is, they are genuine organic conditions but have at least some psychological factor in their cause.

This is, however, an elaboration of the medical model rather than a fundamental revision. Social and psychological causes of ill health – stress, unhappiness, life events – are admitted as agents of disease, or contributing factors, but they are not themselves defined as ill health.

In the light of the most influential critiques of the medical model and the movement, strong in the mid-twentieth century, to include the psychological within it, it would obviously be foolish to present the pure 'biomedical model' as still separate and in opposition to the 'social model' which will be considered next. Modern medicine has moved on, to incorporate elaborate ideas about the various and interrelated causes of ill health. However, though 'Koch's postulates' of specific etiology and so on may not nowadays be taught in medical schools, their echoes still sound in medical discourse and their influence can still be seen in medical practice. Studies of the way in which doctors make diagnoses demonstrate this, while at the same time lipservice is paid to the importance of the 'social'. Moreover, even when social and psychological influences are admitted, this is still a very negatively oriented approach to considering illness rather than health.

The social model

Around the middle of the twentieth century there was increasing dissatisfaction with the dominant model of health offered by biomedicine. The preoccupation with disease and illness made it less able to deal with any positive concept of health. The ideology which viewed the individual in mechanistic ways justified ever-increasing use of medical technologies, discouraging the exercise of other therapies and diminishing the importance (and the resources) allocated to positive health, or preventive medicine.

Notably, the American philosopher Ivan Illich (1974: 918) claimed that medical professional practice was itself a threat to health, identifying the syndrome he called 'medical nemesis':

> Within the last decade medical professional practice has become a major threat to health. Depression, infection, disability, dysfunction, and other specific iatrogenic diseases now cause more suffering than all accidents from traffic or industry . . . By transforming pain, illness and death from a personal challenge into a technical problem, medical practice expropriates the potential of people to deal with their human condition in an autonomous way and becomes the sources of a new kind of un-health.

The ideal that the 'normal' state of the human body was defined by order and homeostasis, and the purpose of medicine was to assist or replace this process, was notably addressed by Antonovsky (1979), who offered an alternative paradigm he called 'salutogenic'. The emphasis on health as simply the absence of disease encouraged thinking about only two clearly distinct categories, the healthy and the diseased. Stressors and pathogens are, Antonovsky pointed out, part of the human condition, and not always 'bad' for us.

Moreover, the 'mirage of health' described by Dubos (1959) is conjured up – we want to believe that science can produce a Utopia of disease-free and lengthy life. Scientists look only for their 'magic bullet'. Antonovsky (1979: 203) pointed out that this means more attention is paid to disease than to health: 'We do not ask about the smokers who do not get lung cancer, the drinkers who stay out of accidents, the Type As who do not have coronaries.' Thinking 'salutogenically' involves turning to a focus on what facilitates health, rather than on what causes or prevents disease – a focus on success-ful physical and mental coping.

Thus Antonovsky developed a concept, 'sense of coher-ence', the components of which were measures of the extent to which individuals perceived the world as comprehensible (ordered, making sense, structured, predictable, rather than disordered, random, chaotic), manageable (with the resources available) and meaningful (making emotional sense). This was found to be associated with health because those who had high measures of these qualities were more likely to cope with situations, maintain their health, and display a psychic 'resistance' somewhat like immunological resistance. The precise measurement and elaboration of this idea has perhaps been overtaken, but it was an important step towards a concept of positive health.

There was some feeling that the most angry critiques of the biomedical model were wilfully ignoring the contribu-tions of modern science to human welfare. However, claims to the unique truth of biomedicine were weakened by some loss of faith in scientific objectivity and a distrust of a Frankenstein technology that could run out of control, and this was part of the modern movement towards a new model usually called 'social health'.

The concept of social or holistic health incorporates many differences of emphasis, though it has to be noted that it is more than simply the recognition that 'social factors' such as poverty or ways of behaving have to be included in a model of the causes of ill health. The social model is a different construction, locating biological processes within their social contexts, and considering the person as a whole rather than a series of distinct bodily systems. The medical model, in terms of specific health risks, does not encompass all of what health means to an individual. The American sociologist Irving Zola (1975: 184) memorably demonstrated this by quoting a physician speculating on what, based on current knowledge at that time, would be the composite picture of an individual with a low risk of developing coronary artery disease:

> . . . an effeminate municipal worker or embalmer completely lacking in physical or mental alertness and without drive, ambition, or competitive spirit: who has never attempted to meet a deadline of any kind; a man with poor appetite, sub-sisting on fruits and vegetables laced with corn and whale oil, detesting tobacco, spurning ownership of radio, television, or motorcar, with full head of hair but scrawny and unathletic appearance, yet constantly straining his puny muscles by exer-cise. Low in income, blood pressure, blood sugar, uric acid and cholesterol, he has been taking nicotinic acid, pyridoxine, and long term anti-coagulant therapy ever since his prophy-lactic castration.

Zola went on to comment:

> Nor does it really matter if instead of the above depressing picture we were guaranteed six more inches in height, thirty more years of life or drugs to expand our potentialities and potencies; we should still be able to ask, what do six inches matter, in what kind of environment will the thirty additional years be spent, or who will decide what potentialities and potencies will be expanded and what curbed?

The social model is holistic and organic rather than reduc-tionist and mechanical. A mechanical system acts according to its programming, its instructions, or natural laws. In the medical model built on the Cartesian principle of the body as a machine, disorders can be corrected by repairing or replac-ing parts of the organism. Holism describes the view that the whole cannot be explained simply by the sum of the parts, just as 'healthiness' cannot be explained by a list of 'risk factors'. Every disturbance in a system involves the whole system. Human beings are living networks formed by cogni-tive processes, values, and purposive intentions, not simply interacting components. This complex system selects its own inputs and responds to the meanings ascribed to them.

The development of this social model has, among the public, been accompanied by a growing enthusiasm for alternative therapies, which tend to rest on holistic principles. Slowly, many of these have been incorporated to some extent into the mainstream model. In particular, health is perceived as a positive state, not simply an absence of disease or an 'average' condition.

In 1948 the World Health Organization defined health as 'a state of complete physical, mental and social well-being, and not merely the absence of disease or infirmity', and this is generally held to epitomize the social model of health. There are obvious problems about this definition, which seems to incorporate the whole of human existence and has been criticized as difficult to measure and impossible to achieve. However, it does draw attention to the kind of multifaceted, holistic and socially conscious definition of health which is most favoured in contemporary Western societies. Recognizing that a sense of well-being is essentially subjective does not make it less amenable to investigation and promotion. Movements such as that known in the UK as the 'New Public Health' become relevant, and the aim becomes an attempt to change the health of societies or groups by altering their environment (making places healthier to live in) or their behaviour (health promotion to change unhealthy lifestyles).

Health, disease, illness and sickness

In summary, in the biomedical model health is obviously most easily defined by the absence of disease, though the model is also compatible with more positive definitions in terms of equilibrium or normal functioning. In the social model, health is a positive state of wholeness and well-being, associated with, but not entirely explained by, the absence of disease, illness or physical and mental impairment. The concepts of health and ill health are asymmetrical: they are not simply opposites. The absence of disease may be part of health, but health is more than the absence of disease.

But the issue remains: how do we distinguish the objective notion of disease and the more general idea of illness? It has become common in English-speaking countries to give different meanings to the words disease, illness, and sickness. Disease is the medically defined pathology. Illness is the subjective experience of ill health. Sickness is the social role of those defined as diseased or ill: as Parsons (1951) first noted, the sick are treated differently to the well, behave in certain ways, and have different expectations required of them. There are problems about this usage, since not every language has equivalent words. But it does have value in pointing out that these three concepts are not the same. That they are different, in English at least, is nicely shown by Erde (1979: 40):

> Consider some of the differences (similarities would show us nothing – or something else) between some of the ordinary uses of two of these terms. (i) There are sick plants and sick dogs, but no ill plants and no ill dogs; (ii) there are sick days and sick leave and sick call but no ill of these; (iii) there is 'homesick' but no 'home ill'; (iv) there is 'sickening' but not 'illing'; (v) there is 'sick society' but no 'ill society'; (vi) there is 'ill wind' and 'ill tempered' and 'ill informed' but no sick of these; (vii) there is 'sick humor' and 'ill humored'.

> This suggests that 'ill' is a much more general word than 'sick'. 'Ill' seems to mean 'wrong' or 'violating the norms' but it applies to a much wider range of subjects than does 'sick'. Nevertheless it has a softer tone to it, it seems less harsh somehow. 'Terminal illness' is not nice, but it is nicer than 'terminal sickness' would be. 'Mental illness' is less judgmental, less accusatory than 'mentally sick'.

People may be ill, that is, feel themselves to have something wrong with them, without (known) disease. Medicine tends to call them hypochondriac if they complain too loudly, but there is more subtle appreciation nowadays that it is very possible to be ill without any – at least, so far identified – disease. Stepping into the doctor's surgery, the person with an illness is transformed into a patient with a diagnosis. Even if no illness had been perceived before, a routine test may show high blood pressure. The patient is then 'suffering' from hypertension (important as a risk factor in heart disease), and the drugs offered to treat the disease are a sign of their legitimated status as 'sick', even if only mildly so. There is some evidence that people so defined may then perceive themselves as having symptoms (as well as perhaps experiencing side effects of drugs) which they did not before – that is, being ill.

Sickness is a useful word for the role that can be assumed by the ill, though not necessarily: it is possible to feel oneself ill or be diagnosed as having disease without adopting the role of the sick person – that is, seeking medical help, assuming or seeking 'permission' to give up one's normal roles or occupations in life or expecting special consideration. People may be diseased, injured or functionally incapacitated without being ill, or without claiming to be sick. It is very common, in surveys of health, to find people with severe disabilities claiming that their health is 'excellent', or the old with many degenerative diseases saying that their health is 'marvellous'.

Both illness and disease imply the potential for suffering, though neither is defined by it. Many who are regarded as ill do not complain of suffering, either because they ignore that which might cause others to claim it, or because their illness does not involve the types of symptom (pain, disability) usually considered to be distressing.

Disease may exist without subjectively experienced symptoms, as in a silent cancer. Moreover, modern medical science produced many liminal states – states which are neither sick nor well, but mark a boundary: potentially ill, but effectively well, in remission but not cured, at known risk of disease which has not yet developed. The American social anthropologist Arthur Frank (1995: 8) described the people he suggests belong to the 'remission society':

> These people are all around, though often invisible. A man standing behind me in the airport security check announces that he has a pacemaker; suddenly his invisible 'condition' becomes an issue. Once past the metal detector, his 'remission' status disappears into the background.

Previously, he suggests, when curative medicine was wholly to the foreground, people could be well or sick. In postmodern times, sickness and health shade into each other:

instead of a static picture on the page where light is separated from dark, the image is like a computer graphic where one shape is constantly in process of becoming the other.

The epigram 'disease (and trauma) is what doctors treat, illness is what patients experience' is often cited. It is superficially attractive but facile. It is true that the process of diagnosis can be seen (often) as the way in which illness is turned into disease, and doctors may try to avoid diagnosing conditions for which they, personally, feel that they have no treatment available. Illness is experienced in time, place and individuality, while disease is abstracted and generalized. Frankenberg (1992) suggests that it is a characteristic of Western medicine that doctors are required to distance them-selves from the current story of this illness presented to them and translate it into timeless disease.

Nevertheless, doctors do treat illness. Individuals do sub-jectively perceive disease. Indeed, much of the impetus to consultation with a doctor is the patient's question 'Is this disease?' And much of treatment is the doctor's answer 'I do not know (yet) but I will treat your illness.' The suggestion that all ill health could be defined as 'that which doctors treat' can give rise to 'measures' of population health in terms of medical consultations, hospitalizations, and so on, which have their own uses for practice or administration but are certainly not measures of health.

How is health measured?

These complicated definitions, of people as diseased, ill or sick, as healthy or unhealthy, and of health as state or status, are woven into ordinary life and usually accommodated. Precise definitions are needed only sometimes, when admin-istrative or organizational decisions have to be made. Should resources be spent on this treatment? Is it legitimate for this person to be away from work? Does this individual come into a category which society has decided to support? We often do want to measure general, overall 'healthiness', however, and this discussion suggests that it is not going to be as easy

as we might think. The measurement of the health of populations – to describe what social or environmental influences
are at work, or which groups of people or types of individual
are more or less healthy – is full of pitfalls. Equally, there are
difficulties for the individual wanting to know how 'healthy'
they are, and for the policy-makers, service-providers and
medical scientists who need to have information about the
health of populations.

The many measures that are currently used reflect the
issues that have been discussed. Some describe health state,
and some health status. Some consider only disease, and some
focus on illness. Some depend on the social role of sickness.
Many rely on the idea of the 'normal' or average, but others
refer to some ideal condition. It is important, in considering
any health statistics, to consider what they actually *mean*:
what concept of health they are based on.

Firstly, as in national mortality statistics, there is longevity,
or *life expectancy*, the chance of dying at a younger or an
older age. This is usually the basic way in which nations are
compared with each other or populations compared over
time. It has the obvious limitation that the fact of life or death
is certainly not all there is to say about health. Also, though
mortality statistics can relate only to the past, and predictions
from past trends can (certainly in the individual case) be no
more than probabilities, the interest of the individual in life
expectancy relates (of course) to the future timing of death,
and the interests of policy are equally usually in predictions.
Moreover, life expectancy is not as simple a measure as
sometimes presented. Life expectancy at birth and life expectancy after the dangers of infancy have passed are very different things. As the years increase, the difference between
groups tends to lessen, until eventually all are subject only to
biological inevitability.

Other measures concern the existence of *disease* –
necessarily, that disease which has already been identified by
a medical system. Following the definition of health as some
norm, it can be measured by standard tests of *physiological
and psychological functioning*. These are the evidence of
health that doctors are likely to apply.

Health may also be measured by the *experience of symptoms*, subjectively declared. This will relate to a definition of

health as the absence of illness. That different individual people – and, more importantly, different types of people, such as men and women, the young and the old – seem to perceive symptoms differently complicates any use of this as an objective measure.

Similarly, the functional model of health appears when health is measured by the *ability to carry out normal daily activities*. An early distinction between ill, diseased and sick was made by Bauman (1961) as (a) feeling-state conceptions ('I don't feel well'), (b) clinical descriptions ('there is something wrong with my back') and (c) performance conceptions ('I am staying in bed today'). In survey methods of measuring health, Bauman pointed out that only the last, performance, is really useful, because feeling states are difficult to measure and clinical states require professional interpretation. Thus an early measure of health, the Sickness Impact Profile, was devised as an elaborated functional measure, assessing dysfunction in terms of many categories such as social interaction, work, locomotion, leisure, intellectual functioning, and others. However, ill health as restriction of activities is still most discriminatory as the 'negative' end of the scale, and selects out relatively few in most populations. There are also the problems of 'normal for whom'?

Health as *fitness* is perhaps a more positive measure which may be derived from tests of physiological functioning, considering the conditions and abilities of the individual without reference to their actual use in daily activities: that is, conventionally, principally their muscle strength, lung capacity, cardiac fitness, and so on. This is, again, a rather restricted definition of total health, but has at least the advantage of offering a continuous scale which can run from the least fit to the extremely fit, rather than the dichotomous definitions of with/without disease, able/unable, or ill/not ill.

Often, the health of populations is 'measured' simply by asking people to assess it themselves. While this is a surprisingly useful measure, in that it does seem to distinguish quite clearly the medically defined healthy or unhealthy, the problem of how people decide to categorize their own health adds layers of complication. Which of all the definitions that have been discussed are they including, with what relative weights? This is discussed further in chapter 3.

Finally, and sometimes as a measure of despair, health is assessed simply as whether people have had contact with a medical system or have been unable to work because of sickness. The problems of interpreting these as 'real' measures of health are obvious.

A conceptual base and associated measures are lacking for positive health. Indicators therefore tend to be distributed towards the 'unhealthy' end of the continuum. These ways of measuring health are also difficult to combine. Is it 'better' to feel well-balanced and happy, even in the presence of disease, or to be without illness but poorly adapted to one's environment? Is the athlete with disabilities healthy or not? How different is the meaning of health in youth and in old age? Measures that describe an individual's health state or status, or characterize the health of populations, have to focus on the different purposes for which these descriptions might be required. To some degree, measures acquire popularity depending on the predominant disease patterns of an era. Communicable diseases and infections lend themselves to population measures of morbidity and mortality. As chronic and degenerative diseases become more important, functional definitions and measures of disability come to the fore. The broad definition of social health leads to more complex combined measures.

Health capital

'Health capital' is a useful way of thinking of positive health in the individual, summarizing all its dimensions and approaching some fusion of subjective experience and that which is objective and measurable (Blaxter 2003). It is, of course, a metaphor: as economic capital is represented by the accumulation and loss of monetary value, so bodily health capital consists of currency in terms of fitness, strength, immune status, inherited characteristics, physical damage, vulnerability, psychological strength and stability, and all the other components of health. The term 'physical capital' has also been used, notably by the sociologist Bourdieu, to describe the bodily state, its fitness, appearance and utility, which can be converted into economic capital. 'Health capital' is a wider term, including this but going beyond it to encompass all the gains and losses in health over a lifetime. A genetic stock is laid down at conception, in utero, and at birth, and in early childhood is elaborated as a basis for life-long health. Throughout life, opportunities exist for the augmentation or depletion of this capital. It is lost by health-damaging events and circumstances, by behaviours such as smoking or unhealthy eating, by the personal dangers and stresses of unhealthy work, by childbearing among women, by the shared experience of particular historical environments such as medical epidemics or economic depressions, and not least by simple accident and the inevitable degradations of time. It can be added to, by positive, life-enhancing circumstances, by 'healthy' behaviour and the deliberate search for fitness, and even by good luck. Eventually, of course, all health capital must be spent, but the timing of this loss tends – always allowing for the ubiquity of chance – to be socially patterned.

The complexity of health capital makes it difficult to use as an objective measure of health, and work remains to be done on identifying all its components. This does not mean, however, that individuals themselves do not have some clear concept of it, and talk of their subjective view of it at length, as will be discussed in chapter 3. And with the ageing populations of many developed nations, and the resulting focus on chronic disease and life-long health, there is a movement towards descriptive statistics of health which can summarize the whole individual and are more sensitive and encompassing than crude measures of health 'state'. An important part of this is the work, to be discussed in chapter 5, studying the life-course statistically at a group or population level, and particularly how health capital is accumulated or dispersed from conception onwards, with the probabilities of good or poor health associated with genetics, birth circumstances, childhood environment, education, work experience, and so on, in complex patterns throughout life.

Conclusion

This is only the beginning of a journey to define the concept of health. But a preliminary observation must be that, viewed objectively, it encompasses all these components – ill health includes disease, and illness, and sickness, and suffering, and physical or mental malfunctioning or trauma. But health is not simply the absence of these; it can be defined positively, and a subjective view may add other dimensions to the concept. Moreover, as will finally be discussed in chapter 6, it is not a static concept. The wider social meaning of health is undergoing major changes, often reflecting developments in science and technology.

Further reading

Bury, M. 2005: *Health and Illness*. Cambridge: Polity.
Dubos, R. J. 1965: *Man Adapting*. New Haven CT: Yale University Press.
Cockerham, W. 2007: *Social Causes of Health and Disease*. Cambridge: Polity.
Erde, E. 1979: Philosophical considerations regarding defining 'health', 'disease', etc. and their bearing on medical practice. *Ethics in Society and Medicine*, 6, 31–48.
Fabrega, H. 1976: The biological significance of taxonomies of disease. *Journal of Theoretical Biology*, 63, 191–216.
Wear, A. (ed.) 1992: *Medicine in Society: Historical Essays*. Cambridge: Cambridge University Press.

2
How is Health Constructed?

It has so far been assumed that health is something which is essentially 'factual', existing 'out there', even though it is multifaceted and may be looked at from various directions, and its causes and correlates may wait to be discovered. Discussion now turns to another view: that health, like all other human concepts, is an idea constructed by human agency.

Health as social construction

Medical philosophers have long pointed out that there is a sense in which even the concept of disease is an invention of humankind:

> All departments of nature below the level of mankind are exempt from both disease and from treatment . . . The blight that strikes at corn or at potatoes is a human invention, for if man wished to cultivate parasites (rather than potatoes or corn) there would no 'blight', but simply the presence of man in a meaningful relation with them . . . Outside the significances that man voluntarily attaches to certain conditions, there are no illnesses or diseases in nature . . . Out of his anthropocentric self-interest, man has chosen to consider as 'illness' or 'diseases' those natural circumstances which precipitate the death (or the failure to function according to certain values)

of a limited number of biological species: for gain or plea-
sure . . . Children and cattle may fall ill, have diseases, and
seem as sick: but who has ever imagined that spiders or lizards
can be sick? . . . The medical enterprise is from its inception
value-loaded; it is not simply an applied biology, but a biology
applied in accordance with the dictates of social interest.
(Sedgwick 1973: 20)

This is an early representation in medicine of the position
known as social constructivism, a major tradition of sociological thought which has had a profound influence in thinking about health. This proposes that reality is constructed
through human action and does not exist independently of
it. There is no suggestion that phenomena are not 'real' and
do not exist without our seeing them and ascribing meaning
to them. But it is only human social activity which constitutes
them as, for instance, health or disease. The social body
influences the way in which the physical body is perceived
and experienced.

How this construction happens is a special area of theory.
In health, a major influence has been the sociological theory
of symbolic interactionism developed in what is known as the
Chicago School in the United States, largely from the work
of Mead, between the two world wars and exemplified in the
work of classic American authors in the 1960s and 1970s
such as Blumer, Strauss and Goffman. Social reality is constructed by individuals interacting with one another on the
basis of shared symbolic meanings: humans construct their
behaviour, their relationships and their institutions in accordance with these interpretations and definitions. Thus health
becomes what people, in interaction, define as health, and
health institutions – such as those of medicine – are the creation of public discourses and definitions.

A weak view of constructivism is that it applies only, or
particularly, to social issues: it would apply, for instance, to
sickness and perhaps to illness, as previously defined, but not
to disease. A 'strong' version sometimes implies that the
world exists only in the head: there are no objective realities
out there. Both of these are easily criticized. The more subtle
position, and the one which has been dominant in medical
sociology for four decades or so (though perhaps more

strongly in Europe than in the United States), lies between the two. This approach holds that the world is at the same time objectively real and socially constructed. There is no suggestion that pathogens are not real, that disease does not exist, that pain is not a reality which can be described in neurological terms and experienced (even if differently from individual to individual) by the sufferer, or that attempts to demonstrate the regularities of epidemiology in numbers and rates are meaningless.

But, at the same time, health, disease and illness are, like every other human experience, social constructs; they are categories which have been named, defined and codified by human beings. The physical body which is their site may be 'given' – by God, by the laws of physical science, by heredity, or what you will – though even this is not absolute, since the body can also to some extent be 'constructed' socially. But disease or health, normality or abnormality, are also socially constructed categories which give meaning to classes of states and events.

What counts as disease or abnormality is not 'given' in the same sense as biological fact is given. It depends on cultural norms and culturally shared rules of interpretation. This is easier to accept in the case of illness, where it would seem obvious that there is immense room for individual interpretations and variations in behaviour: his cold is my influenza. But it must be emphasized that the approach goes beyond illness to include all processes, systems, categories of experience, in which humans are involved, and which are affected by their perceptions, intentions, choices and understandings.

The Polish philosopher and historian Ludwik Fleck was influential in proposing how 'received' knowledge is created and accepted. It is, he suggested, the outcome of a collective process of communication and interaction among 'thought collectives'. These are communities of people exchanging ideas, communities with a centre made up of specialists and a circumference of lay people. In the case of medicine, facts are established by the exchange and circulation of ideas and experience among scientists, doctors and patients. Knowledge is not simply that which is discovered by experts and then disseminated among the public, but something which is validated over time in overlapping networks.

In his book *Genesis and Development of a Scientific Fact* (1935), Fleck presented a case study of syphilis in these terms, and others have explored the ideas in more modern medicine. Arksey (1994), for instance, showed how, in the case of the diagnosis of repetitive strain injury, knowledge is shaped by social and cultural 'thought styles' of different clinical communities. Nicolson and McLaughlin (1988) offered a study of the disease multiple sclerosis, and Scott (1990) showed how the diagnosis of post-traumatic stress disorder became legitimated in the United States.

The 'construction' of disease is, of course, most easily demonstrated in such 'contested' diagnoses, where the biological basis is unclear or disputed. Nonetheless, a constructivist view would claim that it applies not only to these cases, but to disease as a general model.

Constructions of history

It can easily be demonstrated that what has been, and is, defined as health and illness has differed from era to era, and continues to differ from culture to culture. This is in part a matter of increasing scientific knowledge, of course, but not only that: disease has always existed, and always been universal, and biomedicine is a relatively recent development.

> Diseases are no more obvious a feature of the world than any other object of natural enquiry. Even if one supposes that natural kinds exist, separately from human classification, it seems unlikely that disease constitutes such a kind. Phenomena as disparate as hay fever and hysteria are assigned to this category because they inconvenience humans rather than because of any intrinsic similarities ... The rationality of diagnosis and therapy can only be understood in terms of the theory employed at the time, since it is always actors' categories that shape attitudes and actions. (Harley 1999: 417)

Fabrega (1976a) offered an example of the anthropological or historical approach. He noted that the study of ancient populations shows that most of the major diseases now current have always been known to exist. Even if methods of controlling them have been achieved only recently, explana tions and theories about diseases go back to prehistory. Rather than even 'primitive' beliefs being viewed as naive and superstitious, they should be seen as socially adaptive and part of a way of understanding the world. Many primitive peoples, for instance, did not distinguish between medicine, magic and religion, and the power of religion persisted throughout, and beyond, pre-literate times. Taxonomies included deities, powers, spirits – preternatural sources outside the individual. The ways in which they acted, includ-ing forces of the environment, were also outside the individual, though the moral status of the individual very commonly had relevance.

The concept of diseases is continually changing: historians of medicine such as Engel (1963) have discussed how through the centuries the concepts and functions of medicine have oscillated between generalizations – the stuff of science – and concentration on the individual – the focus of medical therapy and what doctors actually do. The dichotomy goes back to the Platonic concept of universals or unchangeable realities, in opposition to the Aristotelian emphasis on the individual.

It is not only that science reflects and reproduces the dom-inant ideas of its time. The somewhat despairing residual definition of disease considered in chapter 1, that it is simply 'what doctors treat', does have some historical rationale. Society gives to medicine and healing as professions the task, in practice, of defining disease. How they perform it is affected not only by the advance of scientific knowledge but also by issues about their place in society. Jewson (1976) notably showed this by distinguishing three medical cosmologies, or schemes within which the medical profession operated, during the late eighteenth and the nineteenth century. In the first, which he called 'bedside medicine', doctors worked within an individually oriented cosmology where they were seeking for causes in terms of personal attributes. The second, object-related, cosmology began with the rise of the hospital, first in France in the early nineteenth century. Patients were no longer fee-paying and, largely, the more powerful sections of society: medicine had now ceased to be dependent on patronage, and control passed from the patient to the doctor. Interest turned to the pathology, rather than the patient: 'Interest in the unique qualities of the whole person evaporated' (Jewson 1976: 238). The third cosmology, laboratory medicine, arrived in the mid-nineteenth century, objectifying the patient altogether as a material thing. Thus changes in the conceptualization of health and disease are bound up with social relationships, and the development of medicine as a profession as well as a science.

What doctors treat as disease has clearly changed over time. For most schools of medicine in the ancient world symptoms were diseases of themselves. Ideas of disease as a syndrome, a constellation of related signs and symptoms, had existed in the Hippocratic school. The anatomists of the later eighteenth century converted the idea of a syndrome into anatomical features of the body, and throughout the nineteenth and twentieth century 'new' diseases were identified as new technology became available – a process which continues especially in the field of genetic medicine. Kendall was one of the commentators who described how each new advance in knowledge of physiology and each new wave of technology added new definitions of ill health to the accepted canon, and how some still survive incongruously. Many are recognized which are still only symptoms or syndromes. Others are based on bacteriology, histopathology, biochemistry and genetics. He offered a pleasant simile:

> In fact, the diseases we currently recognise are rather like the furniture in an old house, in which each generation has acquired a few nice pieces of its own but has never disposed of those inherited from its predecessors, so that amongst the inflatable plastic settees and glass coffee-tables are still scattered a few old Tudor stools, Jacobean dressers and Regency commodes, and a great deal of Victoriana. (Kendall 1975: 307)

Moreover, disease itself changes. Herzlich and Pierret (1985) pointed out that in each age one illness has dominated the reality of people's experiences – leprosy and plague in the Middle Ages, tuberculosis in the nineteenth century, and cancer and the chronic and degenerative diseases of industrialization in the twentieth century. These have become individualized again, in contrast to the epidemic infectious diseases of other times: they are the 'diseases of modern life'. And, of course, this process continues. The 'epidemiological transition', the change from predominantly infectious causes of death (still the pattern of poor countries) to the degenerative diseases which become the major forms of ill health in richer countries, continues and moves across the world. It also marks a change in the social distribution of many major conditions in richer countries. The best-known example is coronary heart disease, known as the disease of the rich in the mid-twentieth century, but now the disease of the poor. 'New' scourges such as HIV/AIDS are world-wide diseases with more of the character of the ancient 'epidemics', but (at least in the Western world) they are seen in a very individualized way. And of course (again, in the Western world) they have become to be seen, through therapeutic advances, as chronic diseases.

At the same time, there is historical continuity. Residues of older concepts of health and disease remain in medical practice and lay thought. For instance, the 'balance' that was the common idea in the Hippocratic corpus was primarily a theory of fluids or humours. Humoral theory, probably of more ancient origin but developed in the Greek and Arabic traditions, saw the body as a microcosm of the world, or Nature, whose elements were earth, air, fire and water. The four humours – blood, bile, black bile and phlegm – were linked to these, and to the four seasons, the four ages of man (childhood, youth, adulthood and old age) and the four primary qualities (hot, dry, cold and wet). Later scholars added such things as four colours, four tastes or the four evangelists (fig. 2.1). Each humour or combination of humours had its own diseases and its own remedies.

This has proved to be one of the most persistent models throughout history. Echoes are left in the English language: bad-humoured, phlegmatic, full of bile, choleric, sanguine. In some non-Western or semi-Westernized medical systems, such as those of Latin America, the distinction between 'hot' and 'cold' disease is still central. In a Western society, Helman (1978) showed how ways of dealing with colds and fevers, in modern Britain, are influenced by the idea of harmony in the classical tradition. Disorders can still be classified by patients – and sometimes by their doctors – as hot or cold,

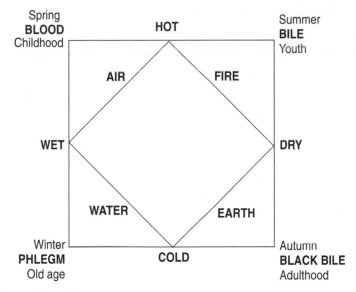

Figure 2.1 Humoral theory

wet or dry. The newer medical concept of germ theory is demonstrated in patients' accounts of colds and fevers, but mixed with this very ancient idea of humours.

Another example is the idea of miasma. Very early in the history of medicine, ideas about the causes of disease, as an alternative to the notion of malevolent gods and spirits, began to include the climate and natural forces. Bad air, or miasma, was the main cause of epidemic disease in the Hippocratic model. In medieval Western Europe, one cause of plague was held to be noxious vapours, miasmas, from stagnant pools, decaying corpses or the exhalations of the sick. As late as the eighteenth century, the conviction was still popular that sickness spread not from one person to another but from the environment to the individual. The bad environments of the slums of great towns, or of prisons and workhouses, generated bad air which triggered disease. This echoes still in contemporary thought, though we now know that in fact infectious and contagious disease is spread from person to person, and most ill health derives from causes within rather than outside the individual.

Constructions of culture

Illness is not only constructed by historical (and professional) processes and the advance of knowledge. It is also, clearly, shaped by cultural and moral values, experienced through interaction with other people and with institutions, and influenced by culture-specific beliefs.

> Nothing is more misleading than to consider the conditions of today's sick as the result of a linear evolution that always deals with the same physical realities, the same notions, the same values, and the same institutions. The transformation of the very nature of the principal diseases over time, the development of medicine with its false starts, its periods of triumph, and its explosion in the last century, the sudden linking of illness and work in the legal framework brought about by industrialization – all of these are examples of a restructuring of illness and the sick which show us that each society has its own way of letting the sick exist, defining them, and taking charge of them. (Herzlich and Pierret 1987: xii)

The definitions and categories provided by Western medicine form only one culturally based set. This is, of course, easy to demonstrate by reference to other times and other places. For instance, throughout human history up to recent times, and still, in poorer countries, the rich have been fat and the poor have been thin. In many societies obesity is attractive and a status symbol. In some pre-industrial societies the wives of important men were given especially fattening diets, so that their body would show that they belonged to the wealthier section of society. It is only in Western societies, where the basic needs of the great majority of the population are met, and 'junk' diets which are fattening tend to be eaten more by the poor than the rich, that obesity becomes a disease and the aesthetics of body shape favour the slim.

It is not simply being argued that 'primitive' cultures lag behind, and have not yet reached the level of knowledge of modern Western societies. There are many contemporary examples from highly developed countries. Norms of what constitutes desirable states and behaviours are highly culturally influenced:

There are, for example, countries where what Americans would call a defect in skin pigmentation is a sign of beauty and health. There are situations (where malaria is of high incidence) in which the sickle cell trait protects populations and sickle cell disease is sometimes said to be the necessary cost of that protection. There are combat situations wherein being color-blind is an advantage for spotting camouflage. There are contexts in which pregnancy is a disease state (*Brave New World*). The culture is (almost always?) at work. Masturbation, homosexuality, blacks' desire to escape slavery and flee to freedom, blacks' poor working habits on the plantations – all of these were each at one time classified as diseases in our culture. (Erde, 1979: 44)

Different societies, all subscribing to biomedicine, may have quite different medical systems: it has been said that 15 per cent of all biomedical diagnoses made in France are not shared with other Western cultures. An example is the common symptom syndromes of *triste* and *fatigué*, the present-day heirs of accidie, the sin of medieval times which became 'melancholie' as the Church lost its power and were subsumed in most Western cultures into psychiatric diagnoses. In non-Western societies many traditional, other, systems of belief exist and are part of formal medicine, side by side with Western biomedicine: examples include China, Africa, India and Japan. This may simply refer to the use of different therapies, especially drugs, but it may present very fundamental differences when (as in, for instance, China or Japan) issues such as the essential nature of life and death impinge on beginning- and end-of-life technology. For instance:

Japanese attitudes to insensate things may offer some insights into the debate on brain death. The way in which machines in Japan are frequently 'animated' comes as a surprise to most outsiders . . . This attitude appears to be a direct legacy from the everyday lives of skilled workers of all kinds, whose activities have long been explicitly linked with Shinto ritual and with qualities of animism. Spirits reside not only in nature but also in tools and other instruments . . . Whereas in North America the thought of being attached in an unconscious state to a machine is humiliating and demeaning, quite different reactions are common in Japan. Rather than vizualize the machine as doing the work for the human, as taking over the empty shell, in Japan some people may conceptualize machine and human as working in partnership, creating an animated hybrid that can overcome all odds. (Lock 2002: 370)

On the other hand, many Western nations are increasingly adopting into their medical systems health beliefs and practices from other cultures. In the United States, for instance, this has included aspects of Chinese and Japanese herbal medicine, various sorts of meditation and healing techniques, acupuncture and many others.

At the same time, there are some concepts, outside biomedicine and medical systems, which are remarkably pervasive throughout all eras and all societies. One of these is the moral framework imposed upon health and illness – more relevant, perhaps, to the way in which health is experienced (chapter 3) but still demonstrable as a cultural value in the medical systems of most societies. Another is a lingering faith in what was once described as magic or ritual, a causal system outside science. Treatment for diabetes, for instance, has been analysed in terms of the 'magical elements' in an orthodox medical system:

> 'The function of magic', Malinowski wrote, 'is to ritualize man's optimism'. Here we have doctors purporting to control diabetes, a metabolic disorder which they know involves a complex of biochemical parameters, through the manipulation of one such parameter over which they have incomplete control. Further, they insist that maintaining 'good control' of this parameter is essential to the prevention or at least retardation of complications associated with the disorder. If they are not convinced they are doing the right thing, then they 'feel', 'believe', and 'hope' they are. They have faith in the efficacy of their ritual. (Posner 1977: 157)

Constructivism and feminism

Cultural perceptions of the body itself can differ and change, as discussed in chapter 3. This is especially true of women's bodies, and the 'construction' of women's health, throughout history and differently in different cultures, has provided a strong feminist theme of research (Martin 1989). In a strictly biomedical model, differences between men and women can be referred to their biology. In a social model, the factually different circumstances of male and female lives may be held to account for differences in health. Differences in health-related attitudes or behaviour might be attributed to 'different' psychologies or cultural identities. Constructivist feminist approaches go further, however, in suggesting that women's health is in part a construct of the system of medicine, historically male-dominated:

> From the language used to describe female organs to the social and political theories of Western society women have been conceptualised as 'other'. Aristotle, for example, declared that women were constitutionally unfit for public life, whilst Rousseau stated 'It is of men that I am to speak'. Human nature as described by these and other thinkers (e.g. Aquinas, Machiavelli, Locke, Hegel) was intended to refer to male human nature . . . Historically, this patriarchal ideology has permeated all social institutions, including science and medicine, where all sfates of women's reproductive lives are defined as potentially 'pathological' and thus in need of 'expert' (i.e. male) control. Throughout the scientific biological literature, the male body is seen as the 'norm' against which female bodies are measured and judged. (Williams and Bendelow 1998: 111)

The thesis is that this is an example of the definition of 'normal' functioning dictated by other than neutral scientific criteria. Men have controlled women's bodies and defined their healthiness. The myth of female frailty was used to justify women's exclusion from higher education until the twentieth century, and menstruation and, particularly, the menopause became medical 'problems'. Doctors supposed uterine and ovarian disorders to be behind almost every female illness, 'from headaches to sore throats' (Ehrenreich and English 1978: 123). Hysteria, the 'quintessentially female malady', has, for instance, been frequently discussed as the typical case of a constructed disease reinterpreted over the centuries and bound up with a view about women's nature and proper roles (Seale and Pattison 1994). In ancient Egypt and in Greece, and incorporated into the writings of Hippocrates, hysteria was a capricious female behaviour caused by the 'wandering' of the womb. Shifting views over the centuries reflected popular and medical ideas of the female character, its moral weakness and susceptibility to possession by evil spirits. In later centuries, with the rise of scientific medicine, hysteria became located in the brain and nervous system, or, following Freud, understood in entirely psychological terms, but still bound up with explanations involving the 'delicacy' and frailty of women. Some feminist historians have suggested that hysteria was in fact a method of protest for women who had no other outlets for self-expression, but others have seen it simply as a response to the frustrations of women's lives in the nineteenth century, or even a deliberate imposition by professionals, more usually men, of a label of pathology on rebellious behaviour. Throughout the twentieth century there was controversy over the diagnosis, now subsumed under a range of disorders not earlier recognized.

More generally, in recent times a feminist approach condemned, above all, the objectivization of women's bodies around their reproductive function, and modern medicine's assumption of control over childbirth. Obstetrics and gynaecology constructed the normal experiences of pregnancy and childbirth in particular ways, especially as *medical* processes to be managed, and it was argued that some of the difficulties experienced by women in labour are in fact due to medical practices and the threatening hospital environment. This led to the movements to resist exposure to high-tech procedures in childbirth and the call for female-controlled alternatives to mainstream medical practice (Oakley 1976).

Illness, labelling and stigma

There are several special topics where many of these themes – cultural and societal contexts, the social construction of what ill health is, health as interaction, the age-old feeling that illness is a moral category and a deviation from some social norm – are specially visible. Mental illness, and chronic disease and disability, are fields where the theme of 'illness as deviance' and labelling theory have been prominent issues.

Labelling theory is a variant of symbolic interactionism, suggesting that 'deviance' is not the quality of the act the person commits but a consequence of the label that others apply to it. 'The deviant is one to whom the label has successfully been applied; deviant behaviour is behaviour that people so label' (Becker 1963). People defined as deviant – different from the norm, usually in a negative sense, as being less mentally fit than others, or having bodily impairments, or displaying disapproved-of behaviour – are labelled, stigmatized and segregated, and the behaviour which is a response to being treated in this way only feeds back to reinforce the label. Goffman, in the influential book *Stigma* (1967), analysed a three-stage stigmatization process: an initial or 'primary' deviation from some norm of behaviour, the negative reaction from others to this, and the stigmatized person's 'secondary' deviance in reply to the way in which they are treated by others. Freidson (1965) developed the concept of illness as deviance, adopting Becker's definition of deviance as rule-breaking behaviour, and taking up Goffman's and Lemert's distinction between primary and secondary deviation.

This is most obviously appealing in the sphere of mental health, where it has long been argued (notably by Scheff 1966) that whether behaviour is called 'mentally ill' depends on how others react to it: what psychiatrists call mental illness is largely simply a response to being labelled as insane and treated as 'deviant'. Less obviously, it can be argued that all illness can be seen as 'deviant', that is, differing from the norm of health in dysfunctional ways. More recently, however, it is being argued that social attitudes to long-term physical illness, if not mental illness, are changing (Green 2009). Technology is altering the former boundaries between able and disabled bodies, and in the modern world of individualism there has been a decline in the stigma associated with long-term chronic conditions.

Constructivism and mental illness

Constructivist approaches are easiest to accept in cases where great variation exists between cultures and societies and organic signs are lacking (as in some mental disorders, such as the example of schizophrenia in the USA and the UK). Mental illness was in fact one of the first areas where these ideas were applied, sometimes in extreme form. In the USA, Szasz was the best-known proponent of the view that the conditions psychiatrists treat did not exist in the same way as organic diseases. He claimed that in most cases it had never been demonstrated that there is a physiological abnormality in those called mentally ill, and their 'illness' simply consisted in behaving in ways which alarm or offend others, or in holding beliefs contrary to those usual in their society. In the UK, Eysenck suggested that the traditional field of psychiatry should be divided into a small medical part, including actual biological abnormalities or lesions, and a larger behavioural part. Another prominent name in this movement was Laing, who argued that schizophrenia, far from being a disease, was the only sane or rational way that some people have of coping with the stresses with which they are surrounded.

It is generally accepted that perhaps this goes too far. Many mental illnesses do exist as biological states, and most are more than simply a reaction to a label. Still, mental illness does remain as one of the clearest examples of how diseases can obviously be constructed, as demonstrated at different times and in different cultures.

Constructivism and disability

The ideas of constructivism and ill health as 'deviance' have been particularly important in the field of disability and chronic illness during the last half-century. Freidson was one of the early influential writers in the USA to point out that, like other stigmatized persons, people with disabilities tend to be evaluated as a category, rather than as individuals. Indeed, two stereotypes are usually involved, both predominantly negative: the label attached to the general category of 'disabled' and that which describes the particular impairment (crippled, blind). Since '. . . by definition, a person said to be handicapped is so defined because he deviates from what he himself or others believed to be normal and appropriate' (Freidson 1965: 72), then labelling, segregating and feed-back processes apply to the disabled as to other deviants. As sociologists went on to point out, there are problems about the concept of disabled people as a stigmatized minority group, and there are spokespeople for lobbies for disabled people who vigorously oppose the idea. However, in practice these processes have clearly been illustrated for a range of visible and stigmatized conditions of the sort first, historically, defined as 'handicap' – disfigurements, epilepsy, sense deprivation. That a state of deviance may be created by the very agencies which are supposed to identify and help was demonstrated memorably by Scott (1966), who showed the relevant welfare agencies for the blind as engaged in '. . . a socialisation process, the purpose of which is to prepare a disabled person to play a type of deviant role' and construct blindness by 'making blind persons out of people who cannot see'.

The distinction between disease, illness and sickness discussed in chapter 1 is paralleled by the efforts of the WHO between their first 'International Classification' in 1980 of disabling conditions and their revision in 2000 to clarify the proper distinction between impairment (the physiological or psychological condition), disability (the functional consequences of this impairment) and handicap (the social consequences of disability). As one may be diseased without being ill, and ill without taking on the role of the sick, so one may have an impairment which is not disabling or a disability which is not, in any particular environment, or if it can be compensated for, a handicap. Disability is a field in which the nature of health as both biological and constructed is particularly obvious. Lobbies for disabled people have been energetic and successful in gaining acceptance of the viewpoint that it is society, not the condition, which disables; disability is

> a relational phenomenon that emerges out of the interaction of a person with impairment and an 'environment' which

includes everything from low income and inaccessible transport to a pitying glance from a passing stranger. (Williams and Busby 2000)

The critique of relativism

The ideas that have been illustrated have been much influenced by the contemporary movements called structuralism and post-structuralism. Structuralism (based largely on the work of the anthropologist Lévi-Strauss) analysed culture in terms of signs, codes and language. Post-structuralism, associated in health theory with the name of Foucault, analyses in terms of power and knowledge, and the way the body becomes shaped, presented and socially evaluated.

Structuralism emphasizes the clear distinction which must be made between biological signs and their meaning as ill health (always remembering that it is not quite as clear-cut, since cultural meanings can easily translate, through physiological processes, into biological signs). This emphasizes the activity known as diagnosis, turning it into a process by which signs and symptoms are evaluated as having particular meanings, and their definition as ill health negotiated through interaction between people. Hence there has developed a large body of work in medical sociology on the process of medical diagnosis, observing the way in which a person comes to be defined as ill and entered into the status of a patient.

There have been various versions of the constructivist approach, the 'hardest' of which – denying the possibility of objective truth – has been subject to criticism. The suggestion that Western scientific medicine has no valid claim to special status, and that biological knowledge like any other is inevitably an ideologically based product of the society producing it, has been accused of not acknowledging the real advances of modern scientific medicine. The temptation to focus on contested diagnoses or mental illness, and underplay the importance of clear pathologies, may be accused of underestimating the burden of contagious disease in much of the world. To this extent the position can be said to be ethnocentric.

There is some argument that constructivism offers an 'oversocialized' view of individuals; that is, it does not allow for what sociology calls 'agency', or the exercise of (however restricted) free will by individuals, the way in which they act upon their surroundings rather than being acted upon. The position called critical realism, in particular, holds that social systems are open to process and change, and people have the critical capacity to act upon these structures.

Moreover, there is the argument that the 'hardest' version of relativism or constructivism cannot prove its own theses: if all systems of knowledge have equal status, then this, too, is only a partial and socially constructed view.

However, in 'softer' versions, to point to the cultural production of knowledge is not necessarily to undermine its practical value. The reality of suffering, or indeed the reality of healing, is not denied. Everywhere and in every successive era, healing requires a legitimated and culturally appropriate system. Harley (1999: 433) noted that 'For exorcist and possessed, or midwife and mother-to-be, or physician or patient' all health-related interactions are effective only in socially constructed circumstances.

Medicalization and the constructions of medical practice

The forms which these healing systems take, and the developments of scientific knowledge which drive them forward, have their own part to play in the construction of health. Certain kinds of practical health systems may shape the development of particular kinds of knowledge, and, in time, the use of new models – from germ theory in the nineteenth century to the mapping of the human genome in our own time – may not simply reflect the social forces driving investigation at the time, but may lead to the selective perception of health phenomena. New technologies can extend health care into conditions not previously treated, and create new 'patients' to be treated.

The 'medicalization' thesis is relevant here: this is the suggestion that the expansion of the universe of the things called illnesses is part of medical imperialism, a professional drive, both materially and intellectually motivated, to take over more and more of everyday life. As Conrad (2007) describes in a comprehensive history of the 'transformation of the human condition into treatable diseases', in the 1970s this was seen simply as professional imperialism. From disruptive behaviours in childhood, to the normal degenerations of old age, things which are simply part of the human condition are transformed into bodily disorders. Now, however, the process is seen as more complicated and ambiguous. To the earlier model of deliberate medical dominance, social movements and patient organizations have to be added. These have been important, for instance, in the cases of alcoholism, eating disorders, or developmental problems in children. Pharmaceutical initiatives are also influential in providing routine medication for large numbers of the population who might previously not have been defined as 'ill'. There is a blurring of medical and social need, since much medical intervention is aimed at altering the individual's performance, behaviour, or appearance. Cosmetic plastic surgery, for instance, though a legitimate medical need in many cases, can clearly be patient- rather than doctor-driven in others.

Indeed, rather than ever-increasing medicalization, there is some contemporary identification of a shift towards *de*medicalization. This is attributed to the rise of the self-care movement, the growth in influence of patient organizations, and the spread of information and knowledge for lay people. These developments are in part commercially driven, and in part the fruit of technological advance. In some Western countries the deliberate policy of governments has favoured self-care and a degree of demedicalization. On the other hand, as will be discussed in chapter 6, some developments in the supply and use of modern pharmaceuticals leads to a new wave of medicalization.

Conclusion

At the societal level, it seems indisputable that, throughout history and over different cultures, the concept of health has been shaped and constructed. New knowledge is one of the forces, and this continues as, contemporarily, new disease concepts arise because of new technologies. Further, it is suggested that, as new knowledge arises, new socio-technical relationships, including the commercial, drive the process on: this will be further considered in chapter 6.

Further reading

Bergholt, K. 2006: *Wellbeing. A Cultural History of Healthy Living.* Polity.

Conrad, P. 2007: *The Medicalization of Society.* John Hopkins University Press.

Freidson, E. 1965: Disability as social deviance, in M. B. Sussman (ed.) *Sociology of Disability and Rehabilitation*, Washington DC: American Sociological Association.

Goffman, E. 1967: *Stigma: Notes on the Management of Spoiled Identity* Englewood Cliffs, NJ: Prentice-Hall.

Herzlich, C. and Pierret, J. 1987: *Illness and Self in Society.* Baltimore: John Hopkins University Press.

Kleinman, A. 1980: *Patients and Healers in the Context of Culture: An Exploration of the Borderland beween Anthropology, Medicine and Psychiatry.* Berkeley and London: University of California Press.

Martin, E. 1987: *The Woman in the Body: A Cultural Analysis of Reproduction.* Boston: Beacon Press.

Nicolson, M. and McLaughlin, C. 1988: Social constructionism and medical sociology: a study of the vascular theory of multiple sclerosis. *Sociology of Health and Illness*, 10, 234–61.

3
How is Health Embodied and Experienced?

To demonstrate that much illness has social causes, and to show how many diseases are constructed by history, culture, or professional activity, is not of course to deny the fact that the manifestations of health and illness take place within *bodies*. People are social beings, but they function through physicality: embodiment is defined as the physical and mental experience of living. In recent decades, one reaction to the ubiquity of the constructionist view has been a suggestion that the body had 'disappeared' in medical sociology and social psychology (though not perhaps in social anthropology), and a call for a more explicit sociology of embodiment.

Embodiment

Turner (1984: 1) began his classic book *The Body and Society* by saying 'There is an obvious and prominent fact about human beings: they have bodies and they are bodies.' He was one of the first to suggest that up till then sociology had been largely blind to the body –

> Few social scientists have taken the embodiment of persons seriously. Any reference to the corporeal nature of human existence raises in the mind of the sociologist

the spectre of social Darwinism, biological reductionism or scientology

– and to emphasize the importance of not separating the biological and the social. He has later considered why this neglect occurred, and how the new 'sociology of the body' came to the forefront. The neglect was part of the legacy of Cartesian dualism – the distinction between the mind and the body, the mental and the material. Sociology had attempted to distance itself from both medicine and biology, and had rejected 'nineteenth century positivism, especially biologism which held that human behaviour could be explained causally in terms of human biology' (Turner 1996: 60). A new emphasis on different forms of the body has derived from radical movements such as feminism, new perspectives on sexual identity, the disabled rights movement, and developments in the sociology of race and ethnicity. As noted in the previous chapter, bodies are of course one of the things which are themselves constructed, and there are shifts over time and between cultures in the understanding of embodiment. In a modern culture stressing consumerism and self-awareness, there is a special consciousness of the body, and technology is one of the things that continues to shift the meaning of embodiment. Shilling (2003) has noted that the sociology of the body draws attention to the fact that, from the individual perspective, 'bodies are always in a state of becoming'. They are constantly altered and shaped by individual actions, by cultural processes, and by biological processes such as adolescence or ageing.

Lay definitions of health

The body has always, of course, been at the centre of people's own experience of health and illness. Lay perceptions of embodiment, and of what health and illness are, have long been a focus of very active research and discussion. As Crawford (1984: 60) said,

> Health, like illness, is a concept grounded in the experiences and concerns of everyday life. While there is not the same

urgency to explain health as there is to account for serious illness, thoughts about health easily evoke reflections about the quality of physical, emotional, and social existence. Like illness, it is a category of experience that reveals tacit assumptions about individual and social reality. Talking about health is a way people give expression to our culture's notions of well-being or quality of life. Health is a 'key word,' a generative concept, a value attached to or suggestive of other cardinal values. 'Health' provides a means for personal and social evaluation.

In its early days, however, the study of lay concepts of health was largely based on a wish to understand why people behaved as they did in choosing health-related lifestyles, or interacting with the profession of medicine. Three broad sectors of knowledge have been distinguished (Kleinman 1980): professional (orthodox, scientific, Western), alternative (folk, traditional, complementary), and lay (popular, informal). Early questions included: what 'folk' beliefs – especially among different ethnic or socio-economic groups – might intervene in efficient and 'compliant' collaboration with their doctors? Why was there resistance to medical procedures, or why were symptoms ignored? What 'wrong' beliefs required attention in health education? The following discussion of lay concepts begins with early examples of these more practical objectives. As Prior (2003) has noted, however, this earlier interest in lay beliefs and the patient's perspectives – part of the historical movement towards a more sensitive practice of medicine – later turned to the use of more radical terms such as lay knowledge or lay epidemiology.

The chapter similarly moves to discussion of how more sophisticated methodology and theory approach the study of the experience and the meaning of health and illness. Boundaries have now become blurred: professional knowledge now includes much of the 'alternative'. Lay knowledge rests on both tradition and medical science. Indeed, it has been argued that, just as it is not practical to oppose illness and disease, so the label 'lay' concepts, though common as a shorthand, is not useful in modern Western societies, where lay accounts are usually filtered through internalized professional accounts. Lay beliefs can be better defined as commonsense

understandings and personal experience, imbued with professional rationalizations.

If, in more recent decades, the approach to what is still
called lay concepts is very much more complex, this is not to
deny that (as discussed in chapter 1) residues of older or 'folk'
concepts are still present in people's minds:

> Treatment of a Cold or Chill is your own responsibility; it is
> your own problem, and is less likely to mobilise a caring com-
> munity around you than a Fever. As in all Hot–Cold and
> humoural systems, treatment aims primarily to fight cold with
> warmth, and to move the patient from 'Cold' (or 'colder' than
> normal) back to 'normal', by adding heat in the form of hot
> drinks, hot-water bottles, rest in a warm bed, and so on; and
> in giving him the means to generate his own heat, especially
> by ample warm food ('Feed a Cold, Starve a Fever'), as well
> as tonics and vitamins, which are also perceived as a type of
> nutriment. In addition, he must if necessary be shifted from
> the 'Wet' to the 'Dry' state – not by expelling or washing out
> the Fluids, but by drying them up. These Fluids are considered
> part of the body, and should be conserved, with the aid of
> nasal drops, decongestant tablets, inhalations, and drugs to
> solidify the loose stools. (Helman 1978: 117–18)

Moreover, their doctors may be complicit in trying to talk in
folk terms, and a patient who presents a list of symptoms is
often given a diagnosis in the everyday idiom of the folk
model: 'It's just a tummy bug.'

Research on lay concepts now goes much further than this
interest in folk ideas, however. It covers a number of essentially different questions. It may be, simply, how people (especially in different sections of society) define health. This is a
difficult question to ask (or answer) in a direct form. Williams
(1996) has commented on the way in which, in health, we
take the body for granted. In illness, this unity is disrupted
and the body becomes separate from the self. Other sorts of
question may be used as indicators: what they see as the
causes of ill health, how they think disease can be avoided,
how they recognize other people as 'healthy', the accounts
they give of their experiences of illness at particular times or
over a lifetime. Different studies, whether surveys or
qualitative interviews, may begin with different interests and

hypotheses, and thus the analytic categories produced may be different: concepts of health cannot be 'reliably' measured in the same way as physiological or psychological attributes. Some common themes arise, however.

Social representations of health

Among the first, and perhaps still the best, studies of lay beliefs were those of Claudine Herzlich in France from the 1970s, influenced by the work of Foucault and Muscovici's concept of 'social representations'. This approach to social psychology – examining the way in which individuals perceive the world as part of the more extensive systems of knowledge that society shares – saw subjectively perceived social representations both as the models which individuals use and as discourses in the public domain.

Herzlich (1973) identified three different metaphors to describe the way in which people talked about health and illness:

* *illness as destroyer*, involving loss, isolation and incapacity
* *illness as liberator*, a lessening of burdens
* *illness as occupation*, freedom from responsibility, except for the need to fight the disease

Turning to health rather than illness, the difficulty of defining health in the abstract is emphasized. Lay concepts were revealed by Herzlich to encompass three dimensions, which could co-exist in one person's account:

* *health in a vacuum*, or the absence of illness, an impersonal condition, recognized only when one becomes ill
* *health as a reserve*, or physical strength and the capacity to resist illness, something inherited or the outcome of a good childhood
* *health as equilibrium*, balance, harmony and well-being, contingent upon events in life, a state often under attack in modern society.

These three are sometimes discussed in terms of health as having, doing and being.

Other work, among different groups of people, has found similar categories. A study of middle-aged women in a Scottish city, and their daughters, both in poor socio-economic circumstances (Blaxter and Paterson 1982), found that health (especially for the older generation) was defined principally in terms of 'not being ill': health was either the absence of symptoms of illness, the refusal to admit their existence, the ability to define illnesses as normal ('at my time of life') or the determination not to 'lie down' to them. Health as a positive concept of well-being or positive fitness was absent in the older generation, and though their daughters were more conscious of fitness few had time or energy to devote much thought to it. A constant theme of these women's talk was the concept of illness as a state of spiritual or moral, rather than physical, malaise, associated with personality and a lack of moral fibre. If, in the face of this view, the experience of illness was inescapable – and, for the older generation in particular, it was – then the obvious residual category was one of health as simply chance.

Another study in Scotland (Williams 1990), of older people, found similar concepts to those of Herzlich, and similar emphasis on the moral and functional aspects of health. Health was defined as the absence of disease, and illness had to be coped with in five broad ways:

- as controlled by normal living, by keeping up normal activity
- as a continuous struggle
- as an alternative way of life
- as a loss to be endured
- as release from effort.

All the work considered so far has noted that the concepts of health derived must be considered in the light of the particular groups being studied. A different type of study has attempted to obtain definitions from large populations, with, usually, a particular interest in looking at the differences between groups. D'Houtard and Field (1986), for instance, reported on a very large survey in France which simply asked the question 'What is, according to you, the best definition of health?' The answers were analysed into a large number of different themes, such as 'life without constraints', personal unfolding', 'being able to work', or 'living as long as possible'. Those who did manual work found physical fitness and the ability to work to be key criteria, while those with non-manual occupations could see health as a more positive concept.

Another study in France, reported by Pierret (1993), used both quantitative and qualitative methods with three sub-samples: residents of an 'old quarter' of Paris, residents of a 'new city', and farmers. The topic was introduced simply by 'I would like you to tell me about health, what it means to you.' Four 'registers' were found:

* *health-illness*, talk organized around health as not being ill
* *health-tool*, an impersonal view of health as a capital that everyone has, the principal form of wealth, to be used as a tool
* *health-product*, health as a personal value, with controllable and uncontrollable factors held in balance
* *health institution*, health seen from a collective and political viewpoint, to be managed by society.

Which of these was favoured appeared to be related to the individual's social and occupational position. For instance, public-sector wage-earners tended to express health as collective and governmental; manual workers saw it in terms of not-illness or as a tool; farmers' illness and risk beliefs fell into a homogeneous world-view based on a cycle of life over which they had some control. Pierret (1993: 22) observed that

> In France, persons' relations to the State, in particular whether they work in the private or public sector, seem to be as important as social class origins.

A large nation-wide UK study, *Health and Lifestyles* (Blaxter 1990), posed a similar open-ended question: 'What is it like when you are healthy?', also asking people to describe 'a healthy person' whom they knew. Five main categories were found:

(1) *Health as not-ill,* defined by the absence of symptoms or lack of need for medical attention, and clearly distinguished from the simple absence of disease. One might be diseased, and ill, and therefore unhealthy, but equally one could be healthy despite disease: 'I am very healthy apart from my arthritis.' This definition of health was found to be a little more frequently used by the better educated and those with higher incomes, and, as might be expected, those who themselves were in poor health were much less likely than those in good health to use the not-ill definition.

(2) *Health as physical fitness, vitality,* a concept very prominent among younger people. Young men, in particular, stressed strength, athletic prowess and the ability to play sports; 'fit' was by far the most common word used in these descriptions of health by men under forty. Women and older men used the word 'energy': sometimes physical energy was meant, and sometimes a psychosocial vitality which had little to do with physique, but often the two were combined.

(3) *Health as social relationships*   Social relationships were also frequently associated with this definition of health, though almost always by women rather than men. For younger women, health was defined in terms of good relationships with family and children; for the elderly, this was redefined as retaining an active place in the social world and caring for others. For example, a woman of seventy-four said: 'You feel as if everyone is your friend. I enjoy life more, and can work, and help other people.'

(4) *Health as function*   Both health as energy and health as social relationships overlap with the idea of health as function – health defined as being able to do things, with less emphasis on a description of feelings. Health as function was more likely to be expressed by older men and women; the ability to cope with the tasks of life might, of course, be taken for granted among younger people. For men particularly, health was bound up with pride in being able to do hard

work. For the elderly, health could mean being mobile, or self-sufficient, able to care for themselves or to continue to work, despite the inevitable ills of old age.

(5) *Health as psychosocial well-being* This category, health as an essentially mental state, instead of, or as well as, a physical condition was, in fact, the most common definition of health among all age groups except young men, and a definition expressed by over half of middle-aged women. It tended to be used rather more by those with higher education or non-manual jobs. It was a very holistic concept: 'happy', 'confidence', 'enjoying life' and 'proud' were words used to describe it, and 'health is a state of mind' or 'happy to be alive' were common statements:

> I've reached the stage now where I say isn't it lovely and good to be alive, seeing all the lovely leaves on the trees, it's wonderful to be alive and to be able to stand and stare. (Farmer's widow, aged seventy-four)

The way in which health was defined thus varied over the life-course in not unexpected ways. There were also clear gender differences. In this study, women gave generally more expansive answers than men at all ages and appeared to find the questions more interesting.

Self-rated health

Another large body of relevant work is that which seeks to understand why people define their own health as they do, when, in surveys, they are asked to categorize it as (usually) 'excellent, good, fair or poor, compared with someone of your own age?' This 'self-rated health' question is an extremely common one, in attempts to 'measure' and compare the health of groups or populations, and, though it may seem too vague and subjective to be of great use, in fact it has been shown to match remarkably well, at the population level, with other more objective measures, and even to predict population mortality rates. However, at the individual level there are of course anomalies, and for many decades there has been study, especially in Scandinavian countries, Israel and the United States, of what these are, and whether they are socially patterned in any way that might be predictively useful. That some people may insist they are in excellent health, when by all objective standards their health would be described as poor, and others insist on poor health for which there appears to be no evidence, may say something about the way in which the concept is being defined.

In the *Health and Lifestyle Survey* self-definitions of health as good or poor were strongly associated with the concepts of health described earlier. The concepts of not-ill and of health as fitness were more likely to be used by those who thought that their own health was good, especially among men: there was, of course, an association with youth (and probably better health) and the choice of 'fitness', but at all ages those who chose this concept were more likely to be the self-defined healthy. Women who offered a definition of health in terms of psychosocial well-being were also more likely to be those who took a positive view of their own health. Differences between social groups showed strongly in self-assessments, with the poorest and most disadvantaged most likely to say that their health was poor, especially in older years. Single parents, those living in areas of high urbanization, and the unemployed were also more likely to call their health poor, to an extent greater than compatible with the objective health measures. States such as depression, and personality traits such as neuroticism, were also associated with what seemed to be unduly pessimistic self-assessments.

It is common to note that by far the majority of people, asked this question, define their own health as excellent or good, though almost everyone can tick symptom lists and most, in discussion, will talk about their ailments rather than their health. This is usually explained as an indication of health as a social norm, a desirable characteristic to lay claim to if one is asked to describe oneself in a single word. More unexpected is the common finding that many people will describe their health as good even in the face of severe impairment or serious chronic disease. This is particularly true of the elderly. It seems that these people are saying 'my health is excellent considering my years', or 'my health is excellent despite my disability.' Health is displayed as a relative concept, highly dependent on expectations.

This is demonstrated in many of the in-depth studies where people talk about their health histories. A self-definition of good health despite evidence to the contrary can represent a positive determination to distinguish impairment from ill health – 'I may be in a wheelchair but I can still call myself healthy.' It may also represent a normalization of health hazards in the past:

> My health was all right. I had diphtheria and pneumonia and all that sort of thing. There used to be a lot of that then. But my health was good. (Woman talking of her childhood in the 1930s in a family of ten children; Blaxter and Poland 2002)

Concepts of the causes of health and illness

A sixth, albeit minority, definition of health found in the population survey could only be called 'health as a healthy life'. It was expressed in terms of health being 'eating a healthy diet, and not smoking and drinking', and was excluded from the previous discussion because it was judged not to be a real answer to the question: faced with this difficult task of definition, some people retreated to answering an easier question 'what causes good health?'. Because it is an easier question on which to present lay views, it is one which has perhaps been asked more frequently than 'What is health?', and one on which there is a long history of research and discussion. Of course, what people believe are the causes of disease and the ways of ensuring health may also say something about their definition of the concept itself.

Remembering the practical service-use focus of the earliest studies (and with the mid-twentieth-century development of the psychosocial model of health also relevant), the focus of much of the early work, especially in psychology, was on whether health and its causes were seen as internal or external to the individual. Historians of medicine have noted that in general causal conceptions of health and illness have ranged between the extremes of the endogenous – the ideas of resistance to disease, heredity and predisposition within the individual – and the exogenous – man is naturally healthy and deviation from this is due to external factors, whether demons or harmful agents in the environment. At various periods and in different societies these broad current of thought persist and alternate. They are still commonly found in lay thought. In the twentieth century, a psychological construct known as the health locus of control, specifically applying social learning theory to the way people explain health and illness, divided people into 'internals', who saw health and illness as the outcomes of their own attitudes and behaviour, and therefore in their own hands, and 'externals', who saw them as the consequences of outside influences or simply chance. The practical importance of the distinction is, of course, that the two groups might behave very differently in relation to their health. Though this simple division was soon seen as crude, and various more elaborated concepts were developed in psychology, nevertheless the internal/external, or psychosocial and behavioural/material, distinction has been a very constant theme.

In a number of studies in the 1980s Pill and Stott (1982, 1987) used these concepts to examine the health beliefs of Welsh 'lower-working-class' mothers. A 'salience of lifestyle' index was used to distinguish between lifestylists and fatalists. Those with a low 'salience of lifestyle' were people who denied any blame or personal responsibility for illness; with a medium level they ascribed illness to stupid or careless behaviour; and with a high level they believed that good health was primarily a product of willingness to adopt healthy habits and comply with preventive measures. The 'lifestylists' spontaneously mentioned taking health-promoting actions and had better health knowledge; the 'fatalists' saw health as a matter of being able to 'keep going' and fulfil their obligations, and relied upon their doctors.

The accounts of the elder generation of Scottish women discussed earlier were analysed to look more widely at their concepts of 'cause' (Blaxter 1983). Each disease or illness mentioned in their descriptions of their lives and their health, and what cause was being ascribed to it, was examined, not in order to consider how 'accurate' their knowledge was, but to trace out the structure of their causal thinking. All the illnesses or diseases they mentioned could be placed in the following categories:

(1)   *Infections and agents in the environment.* The prominence of infections, given that the topic of conversation was often children, and remembering the prevalence of infectious disease at the time of these women's childhoods in the 1920s or 1930s, was easily understood, but the external environment could also include climate, pollutants or working conditions.

(2)   *Heredity or familial tendencies.* These (not always distinguished) were given much more weight than medical science might allow: 'We're all made of an impression on our ancestors, aren't we?'

(3)   *Disease secondary to other diseases or to trauma or surgery.* This related to what appeared to be seen as assaults upon the body, chains of illnesses, anything which might leave weaknesses or gaps in defences. Childbearing left them with a stock of stories to prove that 'A woman's never the same when she's had children.' Drugs, especially the contraceptive pill, were also blamed for illness.

(4)   *Stress and psychological explanations.* These women were very conscious of the mind/body link, and almost any disease could be attributed, at least in part, to stress: 'It's because I am a worrier,' 'It's a nervous trouble.'

(5)   *The constraints of poverty and neglect.* There were undoubted material causes of ill health in these women's lives – poor housing, poverty, physically harmful work. Rather, however, they spoke of neglecting their health, but not in an irresponsible way. Life circumstances made care of one's health impossible: 'In those days, you didn't think about it – you had to be there, you had kids to feed, a house to keep, and that was it.'

(6)   *Inherent individual susceptibility* not hereditary or familial. The sufferer was in a sense responsible for these

illnesses, but given one's personal make-up there was nothing that could be done to avoid them: 'I'm just the type.' There was a common concept of 'readiness' to take disease.

(7) *Voluntary behaviours.* The consequences of overweight and of smoking, particularly, were acknowledged.

(8) *Natural degeneration and ageing.* A conspicuous feature of the women's general norms of health was an acceptance of poor health as a natural feature of the ageing process, and an accelerated time-scale for 'getting on now': 'See, I'm getting on in years, so I'm not really bothered now. See, I'm 47 . . .'. 'Things which 'just happened' were, however, conceptually avoided: randomness was threatening.

Like the Welsh women mentioned earlier, these were a special group, and in both cases it was pointed out that the circumstances of their lives were relevant to their concepts of cause. Pill and Stott argued that what, from one point of view, may be seen as fatalism, may, from another, be interpreted as a realistic appraisal of the causes of their ill health.

Attempts to look at the causal concepts not of special groups (and especially more disadvantaged groups) but among the population more generally have been made in different ways. Stainton Rogers (1991), for instance, derived attitudes to causes from interviews by the method know as Q-sort: that is, asking people to sort a number of statements supplied to them which, as far as possible, reflect the broad range of generally available ideas and arguments about a concept. Distinct themes or 'alternative accounts' were identified, representing the different ways in which people thought about the causes of health. For instance, three of these were the 'body as machine' account, regarding illness, within the medical model, as naturally occurring and 'real'; the 'willpower' account, which saw the individual as preeminently in control, and stressed moral responsibility; and the 'robust individualism' account, which was concerned with the individual's right to choose how to live their lives. All are explained within the interplay between the individual and society, but some models assume that individuals have a choice about their living conditions and that health status is a product of individual circumstances and decision-making, while others see lives as largely constrained and defined by their social position. Stainton Rogers also pointed out that, whether health causes are being seen as external or internal, different types of explanation may be invoked for good health and for bad health.

At the level of a population, the *Health and Lifestyle Survey* in the UK (Blaxter 1990) was used to attempt to derive models of cause. People were asked series of questions about the causes of specific diseases, about what they thought made their own lives healthy or unhealthy, and why it was thought that 'people' – i.e. society at large – were healthier or unhealthier 'nowadays'. The answers to a great many questions were amalgamated to form categories of causal beliefs. In particular, the analysis asked whether different groups of the population were more or less likely to think of health as outside the individual's control or as their own responsibility, whether they thought about the causes of health differently in different contexts, and whether their own health status and experience, as documented in other parts of the survey, affected the way in which they thought about causes.

In the context of a 'survey' about health – and the issue of different ways of 'accounting' for health will be discussed later – 'behaviour', in the form of diet, smoking, exercise, drugs, alcohol consumption, was presented as the major cause of both good and bad health, by all ages and social groups: the lessons of health education about self-responsibility appeared to be well learned. 'Medical' causes – scientific advance, new drugs, medical care, better education – were also prominent as causes of good health, but more among the young and the better educated. 'External' causes – work, or pollutants and poor environments – were less frequently favoured. Stress, pace of life and other psychosocial factors were frequently mentioned for negative aspects of health: almost every disease offered could be caused by 'stress'. There was, of course, a long list of other, less common, categories, but one which is perhaps notable was that poverty and prosperity, general standard of living, was mentioned much more as one of the categories for good health, but less as a source of illness (particularly among the elderly and the poorer groups who might be expected to be the more vulnerable).

As with Stainton Rogers' respondents, concepts of health were viewed differently depending whether the focus was on the experience of health, or on illness and disease. Moreover, people had different concepts depending on the contextual frame. Where the questions were about specific, named diseases, behavioural answers were overwhelmingly predominant: poor diet or lack of exercise, together with stress, could be the cause of almost any chronic disease. In the context of their own health and their own lives, rather fewer gave this type of answer, as might be expected: the causes of their own ill health were individual and complex, and not necessarily wholly their own fault. That structural or economic factors such as poverty or the external environment were crucial was mentioned relatively frequently for society at large, very infrequently in the context of one's own health or illness, and barely at all as the causes of specific diseases.

Health histories and subjective health capital

Health in general is not, in fact, easy to talk about except in this context of life histories. In the national survey of health and illness (Blaxter 1990) over 10 per cent of the population, asked baldly for a definition of health, could give no reply. These were more likely to be the young, and men, who might respond, 'I can't answer that', or 'I just don't think about it.' There is some danger in assuming that this is a negative or uninterested attitude to health, since it may be no more than a lack of enthusiasm for the interview situation. Illness and its causes are easier to talk about than an abstract notion of health, and one's own illness easiest of all.

Using methods other than the structured survey, it is well known that problems are rarely experienced if people are asked to talk freely about their own health or tell their own health histories. Such accounts are a fruitful source of models of lay thinking about the meaning of health and illness. They usually show, for instance, a clear appreciation of the fact that causes are not simple, and that a clear dichotomy between 'behaviour' and 'material conditions' is not sustainable. There is usually a notable strain towards linking chains of cause together in a logical fashion, whether or not the links are sustainable biomedically. For the Scottish women, it was suggested that, although they appreciated that disease might sometimes strike randomly, they resisted the idea that one part of their body might 'go wrong' at one time, and another at another time, without there being any connection. One thing must lead to another: there must be a logical biography. These chains of cause stretched back through generations:

> This fondness for familial explanations, for connecting up the events of their lives, could be understood as a liking for continuity, a desire to give meaning to their lives. Their family histories, together with their own experiences, constituted their identity. Their present health status, including all the emerging problems of middle age, had to be accommodated into that identity (Blaxter 1993: 138).

Heredity and familial patterns were a pervasive theme.

This is clearly relevant to the concept of health capital, discussed in chapter l. For many poor city dwellers a 'healthy' rural childhood was the foundation of their survival, even where the actual circumstances appeared to be unhealthily characterized by deprivation and family histories torn apart by the old infectious diseases. For them, a rural childhood in a golden past represented health capital, though depleted since by specific stressors and events. Working histories and, for women, childbearing were salient for long-term health.

Most reported health histories are bound up, subjectively, with a long and intricately worked-out series of previous events and circumstances. Detailed analysis can demonstrate how people combine the influences of heredity, early life experience, the ups and downs of life events, working and living environments throughout life, and their own actions and personalities, into one continuous story. Many can identify clear turning points for their health, for good or ill. Histories – though of course they may be reordered and rewritten – have a plot, a temporal sequence which give them meaning. Additionally, they link the individual to a social and historical setting, with awareness of the effect on health capital of changing economic climates, gender roles, working patterns, and historical events (Blaxter 2004).

Illness narratives

Narratives about specific *illness* are common in journalism and popular writing as well as research, and have been subjected to more sociological, anthropological, and psychological analysis than the more general notion of 'health'. In recent decades a more subjective sociology, coming nearer to philosophy and literature, has emphasized people's 'lived experience' of ill health. This attention to the *Wounded Storyteller* (Frank 1995) is, to some degree, part of the new sociology of the body. However, accounts of illness experience concern more than simply a physical or mental condition and its causes and consequences, but articulate the individual's situation in the world.

Bury (2001) points out that this interest in lay narratives arose in part because of the growing impact in modern times of degenerative and chronic illness, where 'the contingencies of everyday life reassert themselves, and the subjective patient view becomes audible once more' (p. 267). The loosening of the biomedical grip provides the space for lay narratives to flourish. Also, the promotion of holistic medicine and the value of 'listening to the patient' mean that patient narratives can demand attention. The expansion of public information about illness 'provides lay people with a much greater opportunity to fashion personal narratives that connect the private sphere with the public forms of knowledge' (p. 268).

Bury identified three types of narrative form: contingent narratives, which address the immediate causes of an illness episode and its effects on everyday life; moral narratives, which provide accounts of changes in social identity and help to establish the moral status of the individual; and core narratives, which reveal connections between the person's experience and deeper cultural meanings attached to health and illness.

Frank (1995) has similarly argued that, as acute illness gives way to chronic, individuals need to make sense of their experience, learn from it, 'tell their stories'. Stories do not just describe the experience: they are repair work, creating a new self. Published illness narratives were analysed to understand the cumulative changes in the self found there, and three types of narrative were distinguished:

- restitution, or effort towards cure and the restoration of the healthy self
- quest, or self-transformation into a new self
- chaos, describing a life that will never get better.

Serious illness is a loss of the map that had previously guided the ill person's life, and ill people have to learn to think differently: 'they learn by hearing themselves tell their stories' and by the reactions of others to them. Particularly in postmodern times, people feel 'a need for a voice they can recognize as their own'. Stories are of course premodern, an ancient way of transmitting culture and making sense of the world, but within modern biomedicine the traditional narratives of experiencing misfortune and illness become lost.

> The postmodern experience of illness begins when ill people recognise that more is involved in their experiences than the medical story can tell. The loss of a life's map and destination are not medical symptoms, at least until some psychiatric threshold is reached. (Frank 1995: 17)

As Hyden (1997) noted, since narrative is the way in which we come to know and make sense of the social world, it is important to pay attention not only to what people say – the accuracy or not of the account of the temporal world – but also to how they say it, the way in which they construct this world. Even if these narratives are more about illness and disease, they are one of the sources of evidence about lay concepts of health.

The limitations of narratives

The interpretation of illness narratives is not without problems, however. Accounts of illness, in the forms available for analysis, are interactions between the individual and an audience. Narratives can be first-person or third-person stories.

They also have different functions: to construct the new world of illness or the new identity, to reconstruct a previous life history or, strategically, to explain or make use of the illness. They can also be used to transform individual experience into collective experience.

Illness narratives, like others, have conventional forms: the cause and effect of change, or the 'questing' plot described by Frank (1995), is a common one, in which the narrator emerges through the illness as a new person. Good (1994) pointed out, however, that illness stories have the particular quality of being ambiguous, in that they lack that prerequisite of a story, an end. In the illness narrative there are always possibilities of a different ending: the narrative of health is continually renegotiated.

It is generally argued (Radley and Billig 1996) that we should talk of 'accounts', rather than the concepts or beliefs that narratives display. Cornwell's (1984) early distinction between 'public' and 'private' accounts has been influential. In her interviews, public accounts were those which reproduced what was interpreted as 'real' knowledge as legitimated by expert opinion; these were the kinds of account which would generally be offered in the setting of a formal interview. Private accounts, on the other hand, appeared to arise out of personal experiences, and were usually offered in a less formal setting. This was not simply the difference between 'medical' and 'lay' models, since each could be included in both accounts. Public accounts were 'social representations', shaped largely by medicine; private accounts were personal narratives, which might include social representations to a greater or lesser degree.

Sociology has always tried to give voice to the lay person or patient. Of more recent years, however, there has been a more fundamental return to questioning the limits of subjectivity, in reaction to the movement from 'lay beliefs' to 'lay knowledge'. Prior (2003), for instance, argues that while lay people do of course have information and knowledge to impart, and 'all in all, are experts by virtue of having experience',

> Yet experience on its own is rarely sufficient to understand the complexities of disease causation, its consequences or its

management. This is partly because experiental knowledge is invariably limited, and idiosyncratic . . . above all, lay people can be wrong.

The search for meaning

Some general conclusions may be drawn from the studies, both surveys of health and narratives of illness, which have been described. Firstly, health and illness are not simply opposites. Good health has qualities that go beyond the simple absence of disease or illness and is logically independent of them. Concepts of health – whether described as equilibrium, as reserve or as psychological happiness – connect with other areas of life. Health is, at the least, keeping going, performing one's everyday activities, irrespective of disease, and at the best it is a wholly psychosocial or spiritual state of well-being which, while of course it may be affected by illness, is not necessarily determined by it.

Though the health/illness dichotomy has been encouraged in Western societies since the nineteenth century, by social legislation as well as by medicine, individuals commonly see health as a fluid and uncertain balance. The majority of what may be felt as 'symptoms' fall into a twilight zone which may 'really' be illness or may simply belong to day-to-day experience. Frank (1991: 135) wrote in the eloquent narrative of his own experience of critical illness:

> Health and illness are not so different. In the worst moments of my health I am sick. Where should I live? Health and illness, wellness and sickness perpetually alternate as foreground and background. Each exists because of the other and can only alternate because of the other. There is no rest in either word.

Secondly, the importance of cause in concepts of health and illness is obvious. Asking people to discuss 'health' very frequently soon merges into their accounts of the cause of illness. For those who are experiencing illness, to understand the causes is their most basic concern. As Herzlich and Pierret (1987: 100) noted, medicine has never, perhaps, 'provided a totally satisfactory answer to the questions Why me? Why now?' These questions

> demand an interpretation that goes beyond the individual
> body and the diagnosis. The answer that is given transcends
> the search for causes and becomes a search for meaning. We
> still want to fit illness into the order of the world and of
> society.

People's beliefs about cause affect their interpretation of their symptoms and what they are likely to do about them. Koos (1954), in a very early study in the USA, documented the reasons for the health actions of the people of 'Regionville'. Just as one of these respondents said: 'If I knew how I did it – say, from lifting a bucket of coal – I might not go [to the doctor] as quick as if I didn't know where it came from', so the Scottish women of Blaxter (1983) would say things such as 'If I got another pain I would just take it was the meno-pause again.' These and all the other accounts of health histories are full of people worrying over symptoms, perhaps consulting again or in a different way, because, although they had been given a diagnosis, they had not been given a cause, or at least one which they found acceptable.

A third general point which seems to arise concerns the complexity of people's thinking. Talk about health and illness cannot be expected to be consistent and lack any contradic-tions, because different views are held in different contexts. Descriptions of interview research show that replies to simple survey questions about what they 'believe' should really take the form of 'it all depends', 'yes and no', 'sometimes this and sometimes that'.

A fourth general point is that people's models of health are commonly holistic, involving body and mind. The prin-ciple of 'mind over matter' appears again and again. To be healthy is to be happy, and the causes of many – perhaps most – illnesses lie in the psychosocial realm.

Health as moral discourse and metaphor

Several of these general findings relate to the theme of health as moral discourse. The association of illness with weakness, sin and punishment has, apparently, some permanence, and is associated with ideas of faith, submission, and the redemptive power of suffering.

Herzlich was one of the first to point out that to think of oneself as healthy is to think of oneself as in a particular relationship to society. Proof of good health is proof that one is a worthy and responsible person, and, particularly for working-class people, fitness of the body defines both healthiness and commitment to work. Cornwell (1984), interviewing London families, identified the duty to keep working and not 'give in' or seek help until it was impossible to continue as a key concept of working-class culture. However, in all social groups there are contemporary pressures to identify health with youth, strength and independence – positive cultural values which mean that one is unwilling to admit to being intrinsically 'unhealthy'.

The metaphor of fighting illness, not 'lying down' to it, overcoming adversity, is pervasive in accounts of illness in Western society. Self-responsibility is specially strong among those suffering from chronic conditions. Pollock (1993), for instance, showed how responsibility to maintain health is regarded as a duty not only to oneself but also to families, the wider community and perhaps a higher authority. These attitudes derive from a Judeo-Christian culture stressing both altruism and autonomy. Women, especially, have a moral duty to manage illness because they care for others, but for everyone, moral character is assessed through the response to ill health and adversity. Williams (1993) similarly demonstrated that it is not so much health itself which is seen as virtuous, as the self-discipline which not only responds to it but also produces it. The presence of health reflects correct behaviour, self-discipline, willpower and virtue, and its absence is a sign of weakness. 'Fighting' illness is a way of talking about it which is strongly culturally approved.

It is debatable how far these moral attitudes to health can be seen as a universal mode of human thinking, with many parallels in the anthropological literature, and how far they mirror what Sontag (1979) has called the 'particularly modern predilection for psychological explanations of disease, as of everything else'. Sontag perceived this as something imposed by society on sufferers, undermining the reality of disease, but it may be that it is one more way of locating the cause of illness outside the body.

Health may be seen very fundamentally by individuals as part of identity, but illness is perceived as something both inside and outside the body. To the extent that it enters and takes over, it becomes part of the self. At the same time, it is an invasion. As Bury (2005) suggested, disease can be considered in terms of *attribute* – possibly caused by outside agents but residing essentially in the human body, an attribute of its physical make-up – or *relation* – conceptualized either in terms of social causation or the social process of identifying illness in individuals. It is a common theme in medical sociology that illness is thought about, and talked about, in objectified or metaphorical terms. Disease is 'it', separated from the body, and by extension parts of the body also become 'it', not 'me': 'it went to the stomach'. As Bury suggested, there is inevitably a tension between attributional and relational concepts, and an interplay between them.

Metaphors may range from the moral world, with disease talked of as 'evil', to a mechanical image, with the heart, for instance, spoken of as an engine. Herzlich and Pierret (1987) in France, and Sontag (1979) in America, have written of the way in which, historically, diseases become metaphors themselves: TB of passion, cancer of repression, first cancer and then AIDS in military or even Star Wars language of the body as a fortress and the illness as an invading enemy.

Responsibility for health

Several of these ways of looking at how health is experienced feed into one of the most debated issues about subjective health: on the one hand the question of self-responsibility, health as the consequence of one's own character or behaviour, and on the other illness as imposed, involuntarily, by the material world. There is an obvious tension between the universal wish to externalize and objectify disease and the intensely moral and psychosocial model of health so often expressed. Herzlich (1973), for instance, analysed with great subtlety the part played by 'way of life' in the genesis of health and illness. For her urban French respondents, the individual was responsible for health, while 'way of life' represented disease. Whether people will take responsibility for their health, and how they may vary by social group, is an issue in which those responsible for health policy, health services and health care are clearly interested.

One particular theme of all the work on lay beliefs is the demonstration that how people think about health and illness varies with their place in society. The concepts of locus of control, and lifestylists and fatalists, discussed earlier, are relevant. In general, middle-class people have been said to view illness in terms of mental attributes and attitudes, and be more likely to see themselves as having more 'internal' control; the working class to view health more in physical and functional terms and to lack a sense of control. Blair (1993), for instance, showed how the middle class are more likely to use emotional and psychological experiences in talk about health, and focus more on the role of self, while the working class use more physically located experiences and place less emphasis on personal control.

This may, as Blair points out, have more to do with language and available forms of expression than with fundamental ways of thinking. But it has long been suggested that health has a more positive value for the middle class or more educated (who are the greater consumers of health-oriented products) than for the working class (who are said to be focused more on 'instant gratification' or, more practically, have less time, money or energy to devote to health-enhancement). This has been invoked as a cultural explanation for the lesser use of preventive services by poorer groups of the population.

However, throughout the literature, the mind-over-matter theme is expressed not only by the educated and articulate but also by many in poor circumstances, who might be expected to prefer to blame more the disadvantages which were not under their control. This, and the reluctance to subscribe to the 'inequality in health' thesis, has been tentatively explained in terms of their wish to present their moral identity. Opprobrium is attached, not to having illness, which may be unavoidable and not their own responsibility, but to 'lying down' to it. The Scottish women whose concepts of health were presented earlier were perfectly capable of holding in equilibrium ideas which might seem opposed: the ultimate cause, in the story of the deprived past, of their current ill-health, but at the same time their own responsibility for 'who they were'; the inevitability of ill-health, given their biographies, but at the same time guilt if they were forced to give in to illness (Blaxter 1993: 141).

Their life histories were their evidence that, though they had no great material prosperity to offer, nevertheless they could justify themselves. People in all social groups can similarly be at once 'victims' – that is, present themselves as suffering particular stresses – and at the same time be proud of the inner strength that enables them to cope. Stories of illness in terms of moral virtue, as Williams (1993) shows, reveal the ill person's view of society and their place in it. However, Martin (2000) has suggested that for everyone, not only the poor, contemporary paradoxes are developing in accepting responsibility for health. Ordinary people are now being taught to see their bodies not as a set of mechanical parts but as complex non-linear systems – fluid, changing, unstable, in delicate relationship with their environment. This may leave them feeling 'responsible for everything and powerless at the same time, a kind of empowered powerlessness':

> Imagine a person who has learned to feel at least partially responsible for her own health, who feels that personal habits like eating and exercise are things that directly affect her health and are entirely within her control. Now imagine such a person gradually coming to believe that wider and wider circles of her existence – her family relationships, community activities, work situation – are also directly related to personal health. Once the process of linking a complex system to other complex systems begins, there is no reason, logically, to stop. (Martin 2000: 131).

Lay concepts and health behaviour

While the initial suggestion in social psychology, medical anthropology and medical sociology, that lay and medical views were far apart and in need of reconciliation, may have been left behind, it is still true that lay beliefs have clinical and behavioural relevance. They determine in part when and where someone seeks help for their illness, whether they 'co-operate' with treatment, and how they receive the information that they are given. Also, beliefs, especially about cause, will still have relevance to the way people act – their choices of lifestyle, feelings of responsibility, and responses to health promotion. It is to these ways in which health and illness are 'enacted' that the next chapter turns.

Further reading

Blaxter, M. 1990: *Health and Lifestyles*. London: Routledge.

Crossley, M. L. 2000: *Introducing Narrative Psychology: Self, Trauma and the Construction of Meaning*. Buckingham: Open University Press.

Frank, A. W. 1995: *The Wounded Storyteller: Body, Illness and Ethics* Chicago: University of Chicago Press.

Fraser, M. and Greco, M. (eds.) 2005: *The Body: A Reader*. Abingdon: Routledge.

Herzlich, C. 1973: *Health and Illness*. London: Academic Press.

Kleinman, A. 1995: *Writing at the Margin: Discourse between Anthropology and Medicine*. Berkeley and Los Angeles: University of California Press.

Turner, B. S. 1984: *The Body and Society*. London: Sage.

Williams, S. J. and Bendelow, G. 1998: *The Lived Body: Sociological Themes, Embodied Issues*. London: Routledge.

4

How is Health Enacted?

The interest of clinicians, public health, or policy-makers in these complex perceptions of what health and illness are relates, of course, to the fact that people's actions are affected – their recognition that they may be in need of medical help, their behaviour when they are ill, their health-protective or health-harming lifestyles, and their relationship with their doctors. This chapter, while focusing still on the sick or well individual, considers how people respond, how they enact the states of being ill or healthy. What people think and say – the topic of the last chapter – and what they do may be different things. It is generally accepted that attitudes and beliefs, though they may have associations with actions, are rather poor predictors of them.

A somewhat outmoded term for this area of sociology is illness 'behaviour'. In the 1960s this was narrowly defined in terms of the use of medical care, or was developed from early descriptive studies of etiology at the individual level. Quah (2001: 28) suggests that in fact three distinct terms have been used:

- *preventive behaviour*, or the activity undertaken for the purpose of preventing illness
- *illness behaviour*, or the activity undertaken by a person who is ill in order to define the illness and seek a solution, that is, the perception of symptoms and the decision to seek help

- *sick role behaviour*, or the formal response to symptoms, including the seeking of formal help and the subsequent action of the person as patient.

Preventive behaviour and health-promoting behaviour are also sometimes distinguished: preventive acts include the use of specific services such as immunization, dental care or breast self-examination, that is, health viewed within a model of not-diseased. Health-promoting acts, on the other hand, are lifestyle habits such as taking exercise or eating healthily, that is, health defined more positively and holistically.

The rise and fall of 'illness behaviour'

Perhaps the first impetus given to the study of behaviour associated with health was the realization that most people, most of the time, are experiencing some symptom which they could call 'illness' if they wished. The perception of being in perfect health in every system of the body is rare. Surveys presenting populations with symptom lists ('Have you, in the last fortnight, suffered from headache, foot problems, indigestion, backache, toothache, depression . . .'), or the use of diaries, where people were asked to record every health-related event or sensation, showed clearly that few people could not identify themselves somewhere on the lists, or go through many days without a twinge of pain. Yet, obviously, not all this 'illness' is brought for professional attention. This recognition of the 'illness iceberg', and the fact that there was often little, medically, to distinguish the symptoms brought to a doctor from those ignored, tolerated or self-treated, turned attention to illness behaviour. What determines the identification of bodily sensations as 'ill'?

In the early days of medical sociology, Mechanic (1968: 116) defined 'illness behaviour' as the way in which 'symptoms are differentially perceived, evaluated and acted upon (or not acted upon) by different kinds of people and in different social situations'. This became extended to include not only people's recognition of and reaction to symptoms, and their help-seeking, but also reactions to the illness itself and to treatment, and eventually all patterns of behaviour associated with health. With regard to the beginning of the 'illness career', Mechanic suggested what the relevant factors are, including the visibility, recognizability or perceptual salience of the symptoms, their perceived seriousness, and their frequency or persistence. The extent to which they disrupt family, work and other social activities, and the tolerance threshold of those who are exposed to them, are also relevant. Other factors include the available information and knowledge, the presence of other competing needs or motives, and the availability of treatment resources, and the costs (monetary or other) of taking action.

The model which was much used, especially in psychology, to formalize these processes, identify the factors that influence people to act 'healthily' or seek medical help, and describe the stages of the transformation of perceived illness into disease (by consultation and diagnosis) or sickness (by adoption of an 'ill' identity), was the Health Belief Model (HBM) (Rosenstock 1974) and its variants. The HBM models decision-making according to two forms of motivation in dynamic interplay: predisposing factors and enabling factors. Assumed influences on the readiness to act include such things as concern about health matters in general, the perceived severity of the threat which is being presented by not acting, the perceived susceptibility to this harm, and the likelihood of the effectiveness of taking action. Enabling factors include personal characteristics such as age, structural factors such as the cost of the action, the facilities which are available, and social pressures to act. The first set of factors represent readiness to take the action, and the second determine whether it is actually taken.

Much effort was spent in refining models such as this about individual decision-making, and also in trying to characterize the groups in society who might differ in responses to illness. There was, for instance, classic work, particularly in the USA, mapping out 'illness behaviour' among different socio-economic groups. Why did the poor appear to define health differently, or be less able to follow medically approved pathways, or consult 'appropriately', than those who were not materially or educationally disadvantaged?

Psychological models of health behaviour have been criticized, however, because they seem deterministic and abstracted from social settings. They predetermine what is to be included or excluded in the model and thus can be seen as culturally biased. It has been questioned whether these few dimensions could ever predict the variety of outcomes for different groups in different settings or do justice to the complexity of human experience.

All the factors of motivation and perceived benefits and barriers will depend on the characteristics of the person concerned, and will differ between groups of the population. Perceived seriousness of an infection, for instance, may depend on age, and the amount of threat depends not only on how a symptom is perceived as disease but also its functional importance: slight stiffness of the joints might represent extreme threat to a pianist while being barely noticeable to others. Cultural groups seem to respond to pain differently, and particularly in the multicultural society of the USA, there were classic studies in the 1950s and 1960s showing the variation in reaction to pain of Americans of different racial and cultural backgrounds. Occupational cultures (athletes, heavy manual workers) also shape responses to pain. It is suggested that the major source of 'cultural' variation such as this is socialization – the way in which people are taught, explicitly and implicitly, the values of their social group. The differing socialization of girls and boys has also been seen as relevant to gender-specific responses to illness in adulthood.

The definition of a symptom will also depend on circumstances and health experience. If an experience has once been defined and dealt with, a similar condition is likely to be so defined again. In his early study, Koos (1954) said of a woman in 'Regionville':

> She talked about her own cold and about her husband's hernia, but was confused about what illness really meant. She was unconcerned about swollen ankles and shortness of breath and did not consider them reason for seeing a doctor. Her mother had had swollen ankles and shortness of breath for some years before she died, and had not seen a doctor.

An individual's perception of symptoms often depends to a considerable extent, of course, on the perception of others.

Symptoms affect day-to-day behaviour, and have repercussions on those around. A complex of family lore may be brought to bear on the situation. In some cases, relatives may encourage a definition of illness; in others, they may deny that the symptom exists or that it can be defined as illness ('You're overworked . . . stressed . . . need a holiday'). Negotiation of what health and illness are within the family, or other personal relationships, has been an illuminating field of sociological research. For instance, an early study in Wales (Robinson 1971) illustrated these processes of definition very clearly by asking the mothers of families to record, day by day, every symptom or health event experienced, the action taken, and what the mother thought about it. These were graphic accounts of the build-up of stress within a family, the manoeuvrings around the idea of illness, and the complexities of decision-making. Work relationships have also been shown to be important. For oneself, there is a common natural tendency to rationalize and normalize symptoms if it is at all possible. The possibility of normalization, and the form it takes, will depend on the pattern of life in a particular group. People who do heavy work may consider backache normal; people who work long hours may expect to be tired; many symptoms are unnecessarily ascribed to 'it's just old age'. If a symptom is not too disabling and a simple cause not in the category of illness can be found, it may be ignored.

Person to patient: help-seeking behaviour

This leads to the next stage of the enactment of illness, or what Zola (1973) called the 'pathway from person to patient'. When and why are illnesses found to be appropriate for professional treatment? Even if there is agreement about what constitutes illness, there may be differences of opinion about the appropriate action. In *The Social System* (1951) Parsons had placed the behaviour of the possibly ill person within a theoretical framework by delineating a 'sick role'. This was one of the key points in the contract of rights, obligations and privileges between the ill person, their doctors and society. To gain the right to a 'sick role', to be recognized as legitimately ill, people must conform to the norms of this role. They must:

- want to get well
- seek professional advice and cooperate with it.

In return, they would receive associated privileges. They:

- may relinquish their normal activities and responsibilities
- will be regarded as being in need of care and be absolved of responsibility for their illness.

This was not meant as a description of what actually occurs, but as an ideal-type scenario describing a functional system. Nevertheless, criticisms of this theoretical approach spilled over into complaints that, empirically, it did not actually fit into experience. Chronic disease was particularly difficult to accommodate in this framework, since the patient may not expect to 'get well'. It described an unhelpfully passive patient who took no responsibility. Moreover, the study of the 'illness iceberg' showed that there were other means of dealing with illness besides seeking professional advice, including self-treatment, lay consultation and nonmedical treatment. As Zola (1973: 679) noted:

> Virtually every day of our lives we are subject to a vast array of bodily discomforts. Only an infinitesimal amount of these get to a physician. Neither the mere presence nor the obviousness of symptoms, neither their medical seriousness nor objective discomfort, seems to differentiate those episodes which do and do not get professional treatment. In short, what then does convert a person to a patient? ... 'something critical' must ordinarily happen to make an individual seek help. Given the voluminous literature on delay in seeking medical aid for almost every conceivable disorder and treatment, we might well say that the statistical norm for any population is to delay (perhaps infinitely for many).

There must be particular points where the scales are tipped in favour of professional definition of the illness. The question becomes not why does the individual consult a doctor, but why does he or she consult now? Zola identified these 'triggers' to the decision to seek medical aid as:

- interpersonal crisis
- perceived interference with social or personal relations
- sanctioning by others
- perceived interference with work or physical activity
- temporalizing of symptomatology – the setting of external time criteria for the duration of symptoms or their recurrence.

Early literature on 'the decision to consult', based on an essentially 'medical' model, focused on the rationality or otherwise of decisions. The individually oriented studies of what actually happens in illness episodes showed, however, that what might be defined as rational depends on many factors outside the context of the illness – not simply the objective seriousness of the symptoms and the prognosis, but the importance of the prospective patient's engagements next week, the effect of being formally defined as 'sick' upon a personal relationship or an employer, the whole practical structure of life. Rational decision-making requires full knowledge of probabilities of outcomes, something rarely available to the individual actor. Accounts of decisions to seek help are full of the continual processes of assessment and reassessment, definition and redefinition, which go on before action is taken and a doctor is consulted or not consulted.

Many studies show that stress is an important trigger to help-seeking. It may, of course, be that stress precipitates illness, or that illness is a cause of stress. Possibly, given that symptoms exist, it is stressful episodes which trigger the decision to do something about them. There is certainly evidence that an extra stress does often precede consultation for previously neglected symptoms. The decision often comes as the climax of a building-up of tension.

Moreover, the decision to seek help is rarely carried out in isolation. An early description of the process was that of the American sociologist Freidson:

> Indeed, the whole process of seeking help involves a network of potential consultants, from the intimate and informal confines of the nuclear family through successively more

select, distant, authoritative laymen, until the 'professional' is reached. This network of consultants, which is part of the structure of the local lay community and which imposes form on the seeking of help, might be called the 'lay referral structure.' Taken together with the cultural understandings involved in the process, we may speak of it as the 'lay referral system.' (Freidson 1960: 377)

Modern health systems have developed this process beyond referral to, or from, family and acquaintances. Information is available in more and more sophisticated forms. The internet provides a wide range, from the specialized and academic to lay patient-group sites. Enter the name of a common disease such as 'diabetes' to an internet search engine and millions of entries will be offered. In an attempt to help the lay individual through this maze, which may also of course include commercial material, governmental and institutional sites may be designed specifically to guide the 'person to patient' journey. The availability of alternative therapies, or professions ancillary to medicine, is more and more institutionalized. The pathway to becoming a patient becomes easier in some ways, since accessibility of care is stressed as a policy objective in most modern medical systems. On the other hand, the distinction between person and patient becomes more complicated. This will be discussed in chapter 6.

The patient role – control and concordance

Mechanic (1968: 86) had stressed the positive control which people struggle to maintain over events around 'being ill':

much of human activity and the activity surrounding illness can be accounted for within a framework which views such behaviour as aspects and reactions to situations where persons are actively struggling to control their environment and their life situation. Much of the behaviour of the patient [and, Mechanic added later, of the professionals dealing with them] in defining illness and responding to it can be explained in terms of his adaptive needs.

However, research and theory in the mid-twentieth century still focused on groups and cultures – this behaviour would be typical of this race or nationality rather than that, of women rather than men, of the poorly educated rather than the well-educated, and so on. Particularly, once the 'person' had become 'patient', the individual was regarded passively, as at best a collaborator or partner in his or her own treatment. The emphasis was on 'compliance' with the doctor's advice and attempts to explain non-compliance as irrational behaviour. Was it simply ignorance, requiring better education? Or the conflict of lay and scientific beliefs? Or tension between controlling doctors and their resentful patients, who tried by choosing their own path to retain some control? However, of more recent decades there has been a movement into realization that, while this body of work had some practical importance – for instance, in identifying and removing barriers to medical care, or reasons connected with the structure of care for poor collaboration with doctors – it did not provide answers to the questions about how, and why, individual people acted as they did.

Concepts such as the sick role, the patient role – and even the doctor role – have been recognized as a product of a particular cultural phase of the supremacy of the biomedical model, in which behaviour is seen as response to the biomedical state of disease. As Frank (1995: 11) noted:

> The ill person who plays out Parsons's sick role accepts having the particularity of his individual suffering reduced to medicine's general view. Modernity did not question this reduction because its benefits were immediate and its cost was not yet apparent. The colonization of experience was judged worth the cure, or the attempted cure. But illnesses have shifted from the acute to the chronic, and self-awareness has shifted. The post-colonial ill person, living with illness for the long term, wants her own suffering recognized in its individual particularity; 'reclaiming' is the relevant postmodern phrase.

Much of the literature of the 1970s and 1980s, and indeed some contemporary medical and pharmacological literature, relates to 'compliance', or whether the patient accepts the doctor's instructions or takes medications as prescribed,

attempting to show how degree of adherence to the prescribed regimen is structured by, for instance, age or education. 'Noncompliance' has tended to be seen in terms of
patient error, ignorance or misunderstanding. Actions
which are not consistent with medical advice are seen as
illogical or deviant, and patients are unhelpfully divided into
only two categories: those who do and those who do not
follow instructions. In general, studies have produced incon-
sistent or inconclusive results, with the only certain finding
that the majority of patients do not take their drugs as
prescribed.

Of more recent years, there has been considerable criticism
of this body of work, both in medicine and in pharmacy. If
compliance is defined as the extent to which the ill person's
behaviour coincides with medical advice, this is seeing behaviour from the doctor's point of view rather than the patient's.
It is widely found that it is difficult to divide patients simply
into two categories, the compliant and the noncompliant:
most are mixed, according to their reading of the circumstances. 'Adherence' is a preferable term, implying a more
active, collaborative participation, though this still invokes a
notion of 'correct' behaviour as a standard. The conventional
perspective, it has been suggested, ignores the lay meanings
of medications and procedures and their place in the context
of the individual's life: non-adherence may be a perfectly
rational response to a perceived lack of benefits from the
treatment, undue side effects, or simply the greater importance of other issues in the patient's life. 'Concordance' is an
alternative term popular in primary care, implying a course
of action agreed upon in negotiation between doctor and
patient, which is more likely to be followed than one simply
imposed by the doctor.

Enacted behavour

In view of the complexity of lay ideas and responses to illness
discussed in chapter 3, obviously the enacting of illness is
much more than simply the question of understanding or not,
and following or not, a doctor's instructions.

The understanding of how people do act in illness, including their adherence to treatment, comes largely from studies of groups suffering from particular chronic diseases, including especially diabetes, heart disease, asthma, hypertension and epilepsy. Such studies tend to find that, although many fail to conform to their prescribed regimens, they define this as self-regulation or control rather than noncompliance. The modification of medication has been shown to be used, for instance, explicitly to test the existence, diagnosis and progress of their illness, and to help in the management of everyday life. Over-the-counter medications have similarly been described as tools which patients themselves use for diagnostic and control strategies.

Apart from this work specifically on adherence, and many descriptive studies of people's reactions to various diseases, there is a lack of study of how people enact their illness – how they actually behave – to match the wealth of discussion about how they perceive it and narrate it described in chapter 3. The field is lacking any integrative theory to replace the rejected sick role or passive patient. The narrative method described in chapter 3 has been important in displaying the impact of illness on everyday life and action. However, in terms of sociology, this field is concerned with the experience of illness rather than health, and indeed with *chronic* illness, neglecting acute or critical illness experience. Bury (2001: 283) has commented that inviting people to talk about illness tends to give insights into their experience in limited ways; they may be more concerned with the repair and restoration of meaning than with 'the mundane aspects of experience'.

Nevertheless this work on chronic illness has produced some insights into the meaning of health. Bury's (1982) concept of *biographical disruption* has been influential, suggesting that chronic disease disrupts not only self-perceived identities, but also relationships and practical affairs. Radley and Green (1987) identified four different styles of adjustment to pain and chronic illness: accommodation, active-denial, secondary gain and resignation. These are located on a four-way grid in which the self is either opposed to the illness or complementary to it, and social participation is either retained or lost. 'Accommodation', for instance, means that the self is complementary to the illness and participation is retained, and tends to occur where roles are more flexible and more choice is available about the presentation of the symptoms. 'Active-denial' involves opposition to the illness through increasing engagement in everyday activities. In 'resignation', the self is opposed to illness and social participation is lost.

Another theoretical model, allied to more recent work on embodiment, is provided by Frank. In illness, he suggests,

> people who have always been bodies have distinct problems continuing to be bodies, particularly continuing to be the same sorts of bodies they have been. The body's problems during illness are not new [but] illness requires new and more self-conscious solutions to these general problems. (Frank 1995: 28)

Four general problems of embodiment are proposed, each a problem of action: each has a range of possible responses. These produce four 'ideal typical' bodies in illness, and actual people, of course, present a mixture of these:

(1)   *The problem of control*   The body is, it is suggested, lived along a continuum from predictability to contingency. Disease is itself a loss of predictability and 'causes further losses: incontinence, shortness of breath or memory, tremors and seizures, and all the other failures of the sick body'. Loss of control is stigmatizing, as Goffman (1967) pointed out, and stigma which is imposed by others on the ill represents general social ambivalence over what is happening. Various reactions can be enacted: 'passing' as normal, if possible, or regaining some control by the contemporarily approved method of 'coming out' or deliberately claiming the 'deviant' identity. Strategies vary as to what can be controlled, where, and how.

(2)   *The problem of body-relatedness*   Bodies may be associated with or disassociated from: 'do I have a body, or am I a body?' Frank suggests that modern Western medicine, with its emphasis on images and machines, discourages body association, and this is one of the reasons for the

growth in the popularity of alternative healers. In illness, however, the quality of association with one's body inevitably changes.

(3) *The problem of other-relatedness* Other-relatedness as a problem of action pertains to 'how the shared condition of being bodies becomes a basis of empathic relations among living human beings'. Ill people are both wholly individual in their suffering and sharing it with others. The monadic body sees itself as essentially separate and alone; dyadic bodies exist for each other.

(4) *The problem of desire* Frank expresses this as: what do I want, and how is it expressed for, with and through my body? Ill bodies may come to lack desire, may mean 'ceasing to think yourself desirable to yourself: the ill person fears he is no longer worth clean teeth and new shoes'. On the other hand, illness may provide 'permission' for new desires.

These four 'problems' set up a fourfold typology of the way in which people act out their illness. The disciplined body defines itself primarily in actions of self-regimentation, and its most important problems of action are those of control. It seeks to restore predictability through treatment, displays monadic self-enclosure, disassociates from a body that becomes 'it', and may lose desire. The mirroring body also seeks predictability, but of appearance rather than function, and mirrors its desires on others who are its audience or on popular culture. The dominating body assumes contingency but does not accept it. It is disassociated from self, lacks desire and turns on others. Frank notes that this is an enactment of illness which rarely appears in illness 'narratives', but is nevertheless common, if only for part of the time. The communicative body is an idealized type: it is fully accepting of contingency and associated with itself; the ill body 'constructs its humanity in relation to other bodies'. Frank emphasizes that these four types cannot be either mutually exclusive or exhaustive, and any actual body represents a layering of types. Nevertheless they provide a model for readings of how people act out an illness.

Behaving 'healthily'

Turning more specifically to *health* behaviour, the questions here are: What place do considerations of health have in the conduct of people's lives? What do they perceive as acting 'healthily' and why do they engage – or not – in these activities? Who takes advantage of all the preventive services that may be available, and why do some refuse them? How do people relate to the healthy body? In particular, how do more holistic concepts of health affect lifestyles and general courses of action, not simply responses to illness? The fact that there is growing interest in theory here may perhaps represent some of the effects of the transition from the medical to the social model of health. Illness behaviour, even from the patient's point of view, had still been seen as a coda to the medical model, demonstrating no more than ways in which that model might be revised. Health behaviour, on the other hand, represents the social model, and there is more interest in theorizing it.

The study of health behaviour, no less than illness behaviour, did, however, begin with a medical model. In early work, social maladjustment – of which patterns of health-related behaviour could be seen as a part – was viewed primarily as a function of personality, in part the product of socialization. Early interest was largely in explaining, and knowing perhaps how to change, the attitudes of those who did not appear to value their health, or behave responsibly, or use the preventive services offered. In the 1960s and 1970s there was much interest in explaining the health behaviour of the socially deprived as part of a 'subculture of poverty', characterized by marginality, a low level of social organization, helplessness, dependence, ignorance and inferiority. Apathy and fatalism, it was suggested, might explain the underuse by the poor of preventive medicine in the USA and the low value which appeared to be placed upon the maintenance of health. This subculture was alienated from the values of modern medicine, and preventive behaviour in particular required an orientation towards the future, an exercise of 'deferred gratification', which was incompatible with fatalism. Medical professionals and their middle-class patients shared a rational or scientific approach to health, from which deprived subcultures were excluded.

In subsequent decades, this subcultural model was criticized and gave way to one which emphasized rather the practical barriers to 'healthy' behaviour, and the way in which preventive health care was offered. 'Healthy' behaviour was conventionally defined primarily in terms of smoking, diet, exercise habits, and alcohol or other drug consumption. A great deal of work was devoted to demonstrating that, though knowledge and attitudes to health are undoubtedly relevant, patterns for each of these owe more to the social environment and social pressures and to external factors such as the constraints of poverty, conditions under which lives are led, society's structures of control, and commercial pressures or cultural fashions.

Each of the health 'habits' – for instance smoking, food, weight control, alcohol abuse – is of course an immense topic in itself, in the literatures of behavioural science, psychology, and health education. Theories of *general* health behaviour are less well developed. Some very broad general conclusions can be suggested, relevant to the present discussion. Each of the conventionally identified health behaviours is, of course, very clearly associated with health. They (or any other constellation of behaviours which could be targeted) do not necessarily, however, cohere into a consistent pattern of 'healthy behaviour'. Different groups of populations are typically subject to different patterns of 'behavioural risk factors'. Moreover, the enacting of these behaviours, or their avoidance (in a healthy person), often has little to do with concepts of health. Young men may find other rewards in sporting exercise, for instance, or people may have moral rather than health-related attitudes towards alcohol or drug use. Some people may eschew smoking because they believe it will harm their health, or adopt a particular diet for health reasons, but there are many other factors in tastes, social circumstances and social pressures for these actions that have nothing to do with health. Unhealthy behaviour, in real lives, may have rational causes. Moreover, while some healthy behaviour patterns are the product of better knowledge and education, the association is not necessarily clear-cut. In the population survey referred to earlier in connection with health beliefs

(Blaxter 1990), almost 100 per cent identified smoking as a cause of disease, with little difference between smokers and non-smokers. Among those whose measured body mass index fell into the 'obese' category, 35 per cent said that overweight was a cause of heart disease, compared with 21 per cent of those who were not themselves overweight. It was suggested that the basic lessons of health promotion had been almost entirely accepted, and those who behaved 'unhealthily' were as likely – if not more likely – to be aware of the dangers. In general discussions about their own health, they might of course be given to finding excuses for their own lifestyles or complex causes for their own diseases. They were rarely, however, ignorant of the well-publicized effects of smoking, diet or exercise.

Structure/agency: health as cultural consumption

Although attempts to categorize individuals simply as displaying 'internal' or 'external' orientations in the way they behave in relation to health may now be old-fashioned, contemporary discussion still very much emphasizes the 'structure/agency' question, or the ancient debate about the extent to which people can exercise individuality and free will or are subject to various kinds of constraint. Can individuals act healthily in a wholly voluntary manner, or do the social structures in which they live or social norms and values limit what is possible or likely? To what extent do people choose unhealthy habits, and to what extent are they imposed upon them? The classic sociologist Max Weber, writing in the early twentieth century, provided a theoretical background for these discussions. He identified two concepts: life conduct and life chances. Conduct represents agency or choice, the way in which people voluntarily act. Chances represent class position, the boundaries within which people act, according to their social situation. The interplay of these is a dominant theme because of its practical and political interest in the fields of health promotion and health inequalities.

The commodification of health, emphasizing the range of dietary, leisure, slimming, body maintenance and decoration products which modern commerce and culture provide, and popular media publicize, is a popular theme of contemporary thinking about health. Cosmetic surgery, the promotion of the young and fit body as a fashionable ideal, aggressive marketing of health as a product in the form of 'healthy' foods, supplements or activities, the evidence of pathologies such as anorexia or compulsive exercise – all these are indicted as 'cultural' distortions of the concept of health. This emphasis on the healthy body and the individual's right and duty to cherish it fits, of course, with the individualistic 'lifestyle' approach of much contemporary public health policy. Health-relevant habits are not seen in isolation but as part of lifestyles: the holistic idea of lifestyle – which has become, popularly, a term meaning simply consumption – has replaced the attention paid to discrete actions such as eating this or that, consulting a doctor or not, or accepting immunization or not.

Crawford (1984) was one of the earliest and most illuminating writers on this question of how people see themselves as enacting health in a consumer society. Sixty people living in the Chicago area of the United States described notions of health as self-control, acted out in terms of self-discipline and willpower. Lifestyle 'has become life-denying, with the consumption of unhealthy products, the pursuit of high-risk activities, the sedentary nature of modern life'. Judgement of others and self-blame were recurring themes. Health maintenance must be disciplined within a moral discourse, a shared cultural value of what it means to be a moral person. Crawford (1984: 148) argued eloquently that we internalize the mandate for control:

> Our bodies, 'the ultimate metaphor', refract the general mood. We cut out the fat, tighten our belts, build resistance, and extend our endurance. Subject to forces that lie beyond individual control, we attempt to control what is within our grasp. Whatever practical reasons and concerns lead us to discipline our bodies in the name of health or fitness, the ritualized response to economic crisis finds in health and fitness a compatible symbolic field.

But there are other forces impelling towards release, the imperative to indulge:

> Rather than deny the self, the premise is instant contentment. Social institutions are mobilized to produce a personality structure compatible with consumption. Whereas production requires a structuring of time to the industrial clock, consumption must reorganize non-working time into 'leisure' and 'lifestyle' – a transformation into time available for buying and using an endless array of products. The sign of our culture, projected on bill-boards and television screens, is unambiguous: the 'good life' means a life of consumption.
> (Crawford 1984: 141)

Theorizing health as consumption owes much to the work of the French sociologist Bourdieu, who extended analysis to the explanation of class and group differences in health behaviour. Bourdieu focused on how the practices of individuals – their everyday habits – are influenced by the structure of their social world and, in turn, create that structure. Individual practices are connected to culture and structure, and ultimately to power, through the concept of habitus. Habitus is defined as the ensemble of dispositions by which actions and attitudes in the everyday world are habituated and taken for granted, because they are embodied. A framework of perceptions, formed through experience, socialization and class circumstances, predisposes the individual towards particular behaviour. Thus behavioural choices are typically in keeping with the norms of a group or social class, and the habitus imposes boundaries on the probable forms of action.

Bourdieu (1984) demonstrated, for instance, that cultural consumption in food habits and in sports in France was shaped by class-related norms of behaviour, established through group interaction and internalized, so that both internal and external constraints put boundaries on what was possible. The tastes of workers, within a working-class habitus, take forms which distinguish them from the middle class, who have different tastes. Tastes are ways in which people establish social superiority and express relationships of dominance. The relevance of these ideas in the context of health is that behaviours, even those which might seem most closely related to health, may have powerful springs which arise elsewhere.

Structure/agency: health as self-governance

Health as consumption emphasizes choice, even if economically and culturally constrained. A related strand of theory and discussion is health as 'personal body projects', as individualized self-control in the contemporary 'surveillance society'.

The French philosopher and historian Foucault (1973, 1977) was influential in describing a particularly modern form of governmental power, based on the extension of the 'medical gaze' from individual bodies to the surveillance of populations, requiring individuals to govern themselves, and promoting self-control, responsibility, rationality and self-knowledge. This is not seen as necessarily repressing the liberty of the individual. People become more than docile and passive objects, since preventive health programmes make them a part of their own health management.

It is relevant that the second half of the twentieth century saw the shift from predominantly acute, often infectious, conditions to chronic diseases such as cancer, diabetes or heart disease. The movement from treatment to surveillance, from curing to caring, is in part a consequence. If cure is not an appropriate concept then medicine must, instead, consider prevention and management. Alternative and complementary therapies are increasingly used by both patients and doctors. People are encouraged to monitor their own health status.

Disease is now placed in a wider time-framework: we look to the future, to risk and probabilities of ill health. Illness symptoms may be not simply problems of themselves, but risk factors associated with other conditions. Characteristics acquired at birth, through genetic inheritance or otherwise, may not manifest themselves as illness but may be seen as disease-in-waiting. The incorporation of the social into the medical model means that risk factors are not restricted to the physical: behaviours are risk factors, and indeed activities like smoking are seen almost as diseases of themselves.

As Armstrong (1993: 65) notes, the boundary between the healthy person and the patient becomes problematic:

> The dream of the new medicine has reformed the relationship between health and illness. No longer polar opposites within a binary classification, they have become inextricably linked within a great continuum of health. On the one hand health is contained in illness; the disabled, the chronically sick, the dying and the diseased can promote their health by appropriate health behaviour, enabling reactions and successful coping. Equally the germ of illness is now contained in health. Health has become a temporal trajectory containing the seeds of illness which, nevertheless, can be countered by preventive action, health promotion, healthy living, and healthy lifestyles.

These personal body projects, the new 'inward gaze', aim at what Chrysanthou (2002: 472) has called 'Somatopia', the perfect, imperishable body. The well and the ill are no longer clearly distinguished:

> In Somatopia, a third kingdom comes into existence: the Kingdom of the in-between. We are all at some time dwellers in the in-between, taking our place alongside hypochondriacs, the worried well, the worried-and-maybe-not-well, and the not-worried-but-think-maybe-they-ought-to-be. In Somatopia, where the ideology of healthism is wide-spread, and the rituals of self-surveillance are scrupulously observed, the Kingdom of the in-between is routinely crowded.

In the immensely complex network of modern medical and community care, the patients themselves become 'producers' of health through their health-protecting and -enhancing action. Illness moves out from the body to

> ... problems of coping and adjustment, and medical strategies shift from the pronouncements of experts towards 'informed choice', and non-directive counselling' (Armstrong 1993: 66).

At the same time, political agendas rise, their acceptability fed by some general disillusion with medicine. As Crawford (1977) noted, the placing of responsibility on the individual

– 'You are dangerous to your health' – can be a political ideology which results in blaming victims for their own ill health. People are instructed to be individually responsible at a time when they are becoming less capable, as individuals, to control the features in their environment which harm their health. If faith in medicine is eroded by the non-appearance of the 'magic bullet' and the fear of over-reliance on technology – and, it must be added, if societies find the cost of medicine difficult to sustain – then prevention, and individual responsibility, are obviously attractive answers. The concept of health itself changes.

Further reading

Bourdieu, P. 1984: *Distinction: A Social Critique of the Judgement of Taste*. London: Routledge.

Crawford, R. 1977: You are dangerous to your health: the ideology and politics of victim blaming. *International Journal of Health Services*, 7, 663–78.

Foucault, M. 1973: *The Birth of the Clinic*. London: Tavistock.

Frank, A. 1995: *TheWounded Storyteller: Body, Illness and Ethics*. London: Allen Lane.

Kelleher, D. and Leavey, G. (eds) 2004: *Identity and Health*. London: Routledge.

Lupton, D. 1995: *The Imperative of Health: Public Health and the Regulated Body*. London: Sage.

5
How is Health Related to Social Systems?

The individuals whose ideas of health and experiences of illness were the subject of the last two chapters do not, of course, live in isolation. The way in which a society is organized, its resources and their distribution, have a profound effect on the individuals within it.

> Everywhere and in all periods, it is the individual who is sick, but he is sick in the eyes of his society, in relation to it, and in keeping with the modalities fixed by it. The language of the sick . . . takes place within the language expressing the relations between the individual and society. (Herzlich and Pierret 1987: xi)

Health becomes a political and ethical issue.

Most of the significant differences in health between countries, populations, and groups within countries are not genetic or in any other sense biologically inevitable. They are bound up with that society, its particular place and time, its politics and organization. At the same time, the health of populations has consequences for the prosperity of their societies: for instance, in developing countries, disease can be an obstacle to economic progress. Society has a duty to consider the health of its populations which is both utilitarian and ethical. During the era of the Industrial Revolution in the West, the British pioneer of public health Edwin Chadwick brought to the attention of legislators that the economic cost of the ill health of the poor, taking into account the support of widows and children, was great, but the damage to society went beyond the financial cost. Health is part of a society's capital, and at the same time the health of the population is one of society's responsibilities. The relationship is a reciprocal one.

A functional relationship

Two of the most influential founding theorists on the relationship of health to society were Durkheim and Parsons, holding models of society which are called functionalist. The ideas of structural functionalism were an attempt to account for social activity by referring to its consequences for society as a whole, and to show how patterns of behaviours and institutions are created in ways which contribute to the maintenance of a social system.

The French sociologist Emile Durkheim emphasized the importance of societal structures, norms and processes – things which were outside individuals but integrated them into the larger society. Religion, for instance, was best understood as contributing to the stability of society. In *Rules of Sociological Method* (1985) he argued that social facts are representations of society in people's minds: they are ways of thinking and feeling, cultural and moral beliefs, religious practices and social norms of behaviour. They represent the social solidarity and collective consciousness that bind societies or groups together. In *Suicide, a Study in Sociology* (1987) he used the example of suicide, developing a typology of three major types of suicide: egoistic, where the individual was detached from society; anomic, due to a state of normlessness; and altruistic, a positive and purposive choice. The prevalence of the individual act of taking one's own life was determined by ways in which the individual was tied to the community or society.

The concept of anomie, in particular, proved of lasting importance in theories about health and society. Durkheim argued that human well-being depends on wants being proportionate to the means available by which they might be filled. Societies cope with the problem of limitless desires, as a fact of human nature, and necessarily limited resources by imposing a framework of expectations about accepted conduct which 'permits' only those goals which have some chance of attainment. When, or if, this framework breaks down, goals again outrun means and individuals experience the state of anomie or normlessness, which may lead to suicide. Later researchers and theorists have extended this to consider general effects on health.

Talcott Parsons, influenced by Durkheim and by Max Weber, as well as by early psychoanalytical theory, also emphasized value consensus, social order, stability and functional processes. The social order can be seen as fragile and always in danger of breaking apart. How do societies (for most of the time) persist in a stable fashion? The function of roles and institutions, the ways in which any society is ordered, is to maintain this stability – not necessarily by policing, but by people's internalized self-control.

In Parsons's major work *The Social System* (1951) a synthesis was attempted between the analysis of individual action and the analysis of large-scale social systems. The concept that bridges them is called the 'pattern variables' which structure any system of interaction. These represent the alternative choices which underlie people's behaviour:

- *universalism versus particularism*, or the way in which people relate to each other either on the basis of general criteria, or alternatively on criteria specific to the individual concerned
- *performance versus ascription*, or whether people relate to each other on the basis of what they do and achieve or on the basis of qualities ascribed to them
- *specificity versus diffuseness*, or whether relationships are for a specific purpose or are general, across different areas of life
- *neutrality versus affectivity*, or whether people relate to one another in a detached and objective way, or with the engagement of emotions.

These represent norms and values which are critical, because they regulate how people behave and make interactions predictable, rather than idiosyncratic and random, so that social life is possible.

Systems, it was argued, have needs – both those imposed by the environment and those which the system's own nature require – which have to be met. Using the medical profession as the model for organizations based on professionalism and a service orientation, Parsons analysed the duties and the reciprocal entitlements of the patient and the doctor. For the doctor, the first of each of the 'pattern variables' was appropriate – universalism, performance, specificity and affective neutrality. The analysis of the 'sick role' has already been discussed. It is more than simply a theory of individual behaviour, however: Parsons is describing the key points of the contract involving rights, privileges and obligations which would identify medicine as functional in sustaining equilibrium in society and maintaining social order.

That it is possible for ill health to harm the social order, if only by reducing the capacities of a society's population, is obvious. It is equally obvious that it is the profession of medicine that is given, to a large extent, the duty of 'policing' as well as the duty of curing. The specific 'ideal type' details of the relationship which Parsons devised have, however, often been misinterpreted in later eras. They are not descriptive – 'this is how it is' – nor even normative – 'this is how patients and doctors ought to behave' – but theoretical: if the function of institutions is to maintain social stability, then these are the rules which necessarily follow in the case of medicine.

Responses to functionalism

However, structural functionalism was short-lived as a leading theoretical paradigm in the study of health and society, losing influence in the 1960s and 1970s. The rise of symbolic interactionism, described in chapter 2, was influential. If social life is seen as produced by interacting agents constructing their behaviour on the basis of their own interpretations of situations, if institutions are created by reciprocal processes, then this is not compatible with a functionalist view which appears to relegate individuals to very passive roles. Moreover, the emphasis of functionalism on equilibrium and consensus seemed to favour the status quo and the dominance of the powerful.

Particularly, it was found inadequate to explain change. Conflict theory, with its roots in Marx, maintains that society is not held together by shared norms and values: these are imposed by economically dominant groups. Marx held that people act upon the external world by means of 'labour' and the production of material objects: this is essentially a social process and has to be seen within given historical structures. Within the twentieth-century capitalist system, profit was achieved at the expense of those who provide labour, and, though economic growth may increase the income of the worker, at the same time it increases the power of capital. In contrast to the prevailing view in the nineteenth and earlier twentieth centuries that explanations for health should be focused on the individual, the starting point of accounts of disease was social organization. Risks to health and longevity are graded by social position, and it follows that the cures for ill health lie in change in the social structure rather than change in the individual. Weber added that social differences are based not only on economic factors, on relationship to the 'means of production', but also on status and other forms of influence. Conflict theory turned attention, especially, to the sources of ill health in the economic environment and the competing interests in the organization of health care.

Medicine and society

Thus for decades of the twentieth century one of the major preoccupations of commentary and theory was the relationship of the profession of medicine with society, which is not necessarily the same thing as *health* and society. The institution and practice of medicine must obviously have relevance, however. Later, criticism of the pre-eminence of medicine as a powerful grouping in society, combined with some disillusion about the actual effects or the possible longer-term consequences of high-technology medicine, led to an emphasis on a degree of conflict between the interests of patient and doctor, and on medicine as an 'institution of social control'. In the 1970s Illich, in particular, promulgated the idea that society was becoming increasingly medicalized. Doctors were becoming the new priesthood. Modern medicine was creating overdependence on technical fixes, with more and more areas of life subject to medical jurisdiction. Authors such as Navarro went further, emphasizing the role of the medical profession as the agent of the state. In a seminal essay, Zola analysed the increasing pervasiveness of medicine in terms of (1) the expansion of areas of life to which medicine was deemed to be relevant, (2) absolute control over certain technical procedures, (3) access to various 'intimate' areas of life, and (4) the expansion of medical involvement into ethical issues of the 'good' life. Medicine was, he suggested,

> becoming a major institution of social control, nudging aside, if not incorporating, the more traditional institutions of religion and law. It is becoming the new repository of truth, the place where absolute and often final judgements are made by supposedly morally neutral and objective experts. And these judgements are made, not in the name of virtue or legitimacy, but in the name of health. Moreover, this is not occurring through the political power physicians hold or can influence, but is largely an insidious and often undramatic phenomenon accomplished by 'medicalizing' much of daily living, by making medicine and the labels 'healthy' and 'ill' relevant to an ever increasing part of human existence. (Zola 1975: 170)

In the 1960s Foucault had written in *The Birth of the Clinic* on the way in which the new regime of the 'liberation of the insane, abolition of constraint' in the late eighteenth century was not truly liberation, for new forms of moral constraint, pervading more areas of life, were being applied. Increasingly, various institutions – not only hospitals, but prisons, schools – adopted a form of surveillance over their populations, which Foucault described as 'panopticism'. This all-seeing gaze is not simply an instrument of control. It actually constructs society's view of what it surveys. As Zola (1975: 500) said:

C. S. Lewis warned more than a quarter of a century ago that 'man's power over Nature is really the power of some men over other men, with Nature as their instrument'. The same could be said regarding man's power over health and illness. For the labels health and illness are remarkable 'depoliticizers' of an issue. By locating the source and the treatment of problems in an individual, other levels of intervention are effectively closed. By the very acceptance of a specific behaviour as an 'illness' and the definition of illness as an undesirable state the issue becomes not whether to deal with a particular problem but how and when. Thus, the debate over homosexuality, drugs, abortion, becomes focussed on the degree of sickness attached to the phenomenon in question or the extent of health risk involved. And the more principled, more perplexing, or even moral issue of what freedom should an individual have over his/her own body is shunted aside.

It is clinical knowledge which gives medicine power and authority. Foucault noted how 'becoming a patient' meant becoming vulnerable, a diminution of social and political status. The doctor develops a discourse which collapses speech (*parole*) and observation (*surveillance*) into one action, the gaze (*regard*): an act of objectification. He also described the 'medicine of the species' (diagnosis and treatment of disease, which makes the body an object for observation and treatment by the medical profession) and 'medicine of social spaces' (prevention, which makes public health subject to regulation by the state).

Armstrong (1993) has written of how, during the twentieth century, the main change in the nature of the 'clinical gaze' was the extension of surveillance from the interior of the body, the individual anatomy, to relationships or the social body. For instance, TB, previously seen as a disease of individual bodies in disadvantaged environments, became a disease of contact. Nineteenth-century public health had been concerned with sanitation, with the dangers of the environment. With the rise of surveillance medicine, the focus of epidemiology began to shift from the environment to the mode of transmission between people. At the same time the 'atlas' which Foucault described as codifying and interpreting the body in the late eighteenth century becomes a new way of seeing it:

The atlas is therefore a means of interpreting the body, of seeing its form and nature and establishing its reality. The modern body of the patient, which has become the unquestioned object of clinical practice, is a product of the exercise of those same clinical techniques. The clinical gaze, encompassing all the techniques, languages and assumptions of modern medicine, establishes by its authority and penetration an observable and analysable space in which is crystallized that apparently solid figure of the discrete human body. (Armstrong 1993: 56)

With the socio-medical survey as its tool, it became possible for public health to collate and assess population information, and define the 'normal' in terms of the average, using standardized indicators of mental and physical health (Armstrong 1995). More and more attributes of the individual, and ever-widening areas of human life, could be brought into the net of surveillance.

Health, economic development and social organization

Health and society do not interact only through the professions of public health and clinical medicine. A separate strand of theory relates to the relationship of economic development to health. This turns attention from the possibly oppressive effects of the systems and science of medicine to its obviously positive successes, together with economic development, in prolonging human lives.

For comparison over time or between different nations, average years of life expectancy is the most common measure, since this can be clearly defined. (As discussed in chapter 1, all the available ways in which *illness* might be measured or healthiness compared are problematic, as they are so affected by cultural and system differences.) Obviously, in the long term the health status of populations increases with economic development and the fact that life expectancy at birth differs between regions of the world needs no emphasis. For instance, in 2008 life expectancy in Japan or Sweden was more than eighty years, in North America seventy-eight years, in Brazil seventy-two years, in India sixty-three years, and in several sub-Saharan African countries less than fifty years. This is health defined in the simplest terms, and economic development shown to affect health in the starkest way.

In the developed world, one of the most striking features of population health is that, in general, life expectancy continues to improve from one generation to the next. In 1900, the UK expectancy of life at birth of men was forty-four years, in 1950–2 sixty-six years, in 1991–3 almost seventy-four years, and in 2005–7 over seventy-seven. Now two or three years are added to life expectancy at birth with each decade that passes. It is not that old people live longer, but that more people live to be old, since death rates in infancy are particularly reduced. As Wilkinson (1996) noted, a rapid and sustained rise in living standards dates back to at least the middle of the nineteenth century, and for the bulk of the population, the stranglehold on health of the absolute standard of living has been overcome. Wilkinson goes on to point out, however, that, though the curve relating the average life expectancy of different countries to their gross national product per capita (or income per capita) is very steep at low levels of income, it becomes flatter, in each historical period, as standards of living rise. This is not because some absolute biological limit to life expectancy is being reached, since each stage of development shifts the life expectancy curve upwards. It does suggest, however, in richer countries,

> . . . the attainment among the majority of the population of a minimum real material standard of living, above which further increases in personal subsistence no longer provide the key to further increases in health. (Wilkinson 1996:48)

Part of the explanation for the associations between development and health are obvious: not only this 'real material standard of living', but the changing of disease patterns, especially the relative disappearance of infectious disease, the advances of public health and hygiene, and also the nonmaterial benefits – education, for instance – associated with economic development. How much is due to the advances of medical science or the universal availability of modern medicine is problematic. McKeown et al. (1975), notably, pointed out that the vast bulk of the decline in mortality from infectious disease came before the relevant advances of medicine – immunization, or effective forms of treatment – and suggested that increases in the standard of living, especially in housing and nutrition, must take the greatest credit for longer life. More recently, however, it has been pointed out that the thesis that medical science is not responsible for advances in population health is not inevitably true: there are examples where decreases in death rates can be shown to be the effect of specific medical advances.

What is clear, however, is that, once a certain stage of development has been reached, systems of medicine – the proportion of gross national product spent on doctors and hospitals, for instance, or the way in which medical care is organized – are not very relevant to any differences between nations in the longevity of their populations.

The downside of economic development

Economic development obviously does bring with it benefits. On the other hand, the way in which it brings particular forms of harm to health is another of the major streams of thinking and research in modern times. Life expectancy is, in fact, only one measure of health. Longer life means a greater likelihood of degenerative disease, so that the actual experience of ill health may in fact increase.

Because industrialization has been, historically, associated with development and with rising standards of living, epidemiologists and historians have studied particularly who gained and who lost in the process of industrialization, and how some of its obvious health-harming effects were distributed. There is some evidence that, in the United States in the mid-nineteenth century, even life expectancy declined and attained height – a standard indicator of the health of populations, within genetic limits – deteriorated. Suggested explanations were the easier spread of disease, and the emergence of cycles of prosperity and slump. During the early and mid-nineteenth century in the UK, deterioration in health was ascribed to urbanization and the deprivations of the urban poor. In 1842 Edwin Chadwick reported on *The Sanitary Conditions of the Labouring Population of Great Britain*, documenting their disadvantaged health and noting:

> We have seen that there are whole streets of houses, composing some of the wynds of Glasgow and Edinburgh, and great numbers of the courts in London, and the older towns in England, in which the condition of every inhabited room, and the physical condition of the inmates, is even more horrible than the worst of the dungeons that [prison reformer] Howard ever visited . . .

The health effects were unknown, or until then at least unacknowledged and unrecorded:

> The statements of the condition of considerable proportions of the labouring population of the towns into which the present inquiries have been carried have been received with surprise by persons of the wealthier classes living in the immediate vicinity, to whom the facts were as strange as if they related to foreigners or the natives of an unknown country. When Dr Arnott with myself and others were examining the abodes of the poorest classes in Glasgow and Edinburgh, we were regarded with astonishment; and it was frequently declared by the inmates, that they had never for many years witnessed the approach or the presence of persons of that condition near them.

A new perception of ill health as closely associated with poverty was being promulgated. Engels argued in the key early text in the Marxist tradition, *The Condition of the Working Classes in England*, that poor health is a direct outcome of capitalism's pursuit of profit. Half a century later in 1901 the social reformer Rowntree studied the city of York and noted the 'terrible waste of life' in the poorer areas, where more than a quarter of children died in their first year. Similar declines in the economic circumstances of groups of the population, with effects on health, are known for France, the Netherlands and other European countries.

This is health harm as a by-product of industrialization. More generally, it is argued that, in capitalist modes of operation, the health needs of the population will inevitably at some times come into conflict with the requirements of the capitalist system. Contemporarily, this strand of explanation is represented by the examination of historical trends, associating population health with particular periods of economic depression. At the level of individuals within a society, there is study of the effect of unemployment, local recession or economic uncertainty. In the UK, prospective studies of workplaces threatened with change, or workers becoming unemployed, have shown clear evidence of the way in which health is likely to deteriorate – whether through material hardship, changes in behaviour or psychosocial effects.

An associated topic of research and discussion is whether a society's welfare systems can provide effective buffers, with effects on health, against national, local or personal economic failure. It has sometimes been suggested that the better health of the Nordic states (as measured by longevity), compared with some other countries at the same stage of development, can be ascribed to their well-developed institutional arrangements, including social benefits and welfare services. Research on a recent period of recession suggested that within each of these countries the prevalence of ill health remained at similar levels, and the welfare services (which, though cut during the recession, broadly remained) may have acted as a buffer against the structural pressures (Lahelma et al. 2002).

That economic and political developments do have clear effects on population health has been demonstrated particularly by the recent history of the former Soviet Union and the countries of the former communist bloc (McKee 2001). These underwent extreme social and economic shock, inflation, unemployment, stress and insecurity, and experienced actual increases in mortality, though in some countries these have to some extent reversed. However, especially in Russia and the European countries of the former Soviet Union, a long-lasting health crisis appears to have resulted. Between 1987 and 1994, life expectancy of adult males fell by over seven years to 57.5 years. It rose again in 1998 to 61.3 years, but subsequently declined again. Various immediate causes have been discussed, including environmental degradation, crime and violence, alcohol consumption, and growing economic inequality. More fundamentally, major explanations have been seen as changes in the socio-political environment, including exclusion from the political process, high levels of frustration with social change, weakening of social networks and support systems, and a perceived lack of control over life (Bobak et al. 1998). In general terms this is seen as one of the clearest examples of the relationships between health and the economic and social organization of societies.

The concept of inequality in health

A basic corollary of the politico-economic view of the relationship of health to social structure is that the nature of the labour process in capitalism necessarily creates inequalities between sections of the population. 'Inequality' in health, in terms of comparing social groups within societies, has been one of the most active areas of research and discussion for some three or four decades. In high-income countries, where most people have relatively good access to adequate food, shelter, and sanitation as basic necessities of life, important environmental factors which determine health are now related to the social structures in which people's lives are embedded. In less-developed countries, with their burden of disease preventable by public health measures, the importance of social inequality is less apparent, but here too household income and education are strongly correlated with health outcomes: it is still true that the affluent flourish and the less affluent do not. Everywhere, inequalities, both between nations and within them, are important. The debate about their effects and causes not only contributes to the understanding of health and society: it also reflects back upon some of the issues surrounding the concept of health itself.

What 'inequality' means in this context requires some consideration. Obviously, simple equality in health is impossible of attainment: differences in health, associated with genetic inheritance, gender, geography and pure chance (and of course age) are part of the human condition. Are we saying simply that people differ? Surveys of the views of ordinary people about health inequalities have tended to demonstrate a sturdy doubt about any structured relationship between social position and health: we are all individuals, and must all die, and

> I couldn't think it makes any difference myself. I mean, it's like people with money, they get the same illnesses as we get. So I shouldn't think it would make any difference whether you are skilled or unskilled. (Working-class woman, quoted by Calnan 1987)

Or does inequality in health mean simply that there is inequality in all the things in life which might sustain health – food, living environments, medical care – and that the issue is only one of the extent of extreme economic deprivation? The fact that in almost all circumstances a continuous gradient in health is found, running from the least to the most advantaged, has been taken as evidence that social equality affects all groups of a population, and is not just a phenomenon associated with deprivation.

In effect, the term 'inequality in health' has come to mean a special sort of difference, in the context of social epidemiology and health policy. It can be defined as that difference in health between individuals or groups which is:

- socially determined, that is, due not to biological but to social factors. There are typical health differences between racial groups, for instance, which are biologically determined: they are not necessarily inequalities, though there may be other dimensions of race (discrimination and stress, provision and use of services) which are.
- felt to be unjust, inequitable or immoral: there are some typical differences in social groups which are viewed as their own choice, and not necessarily unjust. Inequalities tend always to have a moral dimension, but what is felt to be unfair is relative and susceptible to change.
- held not to be inevitable, that is, they could, within current technologies and knowledge, be alleviated. Thus, as technology advances, 'inequalities' become differently defined. As their cause is uncovered and cure or avoidance become possible, so they become not acts of God but susceptible to human intervention.

Thus the concept of inequality in health in Western societies is obviously a highly constructed one, depending on the social organization of societies, on ethical positions, and on the progress of science. It is obviously much more than equity of health-service provision, since, even if health-service supply were the crucial determinant of good health, equal services might result in very unequal health. 'Equity of provision for equal need' is a common way in which policy attempts to find a services-relevant description, but obviously even this cannot guarantee the abolition of inequalities in health.

The measurement of inequalities in health is as problematic as the measures of 'health' itself considered in chapter 1, with added layers of complexity caused by the need to define the social characteristics of the groups being compared. The measure which is most often used, for populations, for the purposes of comparison over time or between nations, is, again, rates of death, or life expectancy. The inequalities field has perhaps been responsible for reinforcing the emphasis on this as a measure of health. However, as noted in chapter 1, mortality rates inevitably relate to causes in the past, and can only be measured retrospectively. Life expectancy at birth and life expectancy at, say, age sixty-five may be differently patterned, depending – for instance – on the importance in any specific group or society of infant deaths. Longevity may imply greater incapacity and dependence overall. For these reasons, 'years of healthy life', or 'potential years of life lost (PYLL) before the age of seventy' are measures which are used, the latter because investigating the causes of premature mortality may be particularly useful in pointing to specific areas of potential intervention.

Inequalities may be measured in relative or in absolute terms – that is, as (for instance) the ratio of death rates in the least favourable group, whether social, geographical, or ethnic, to those in the most favourable, or in terms of simple difference in years or life expectancy between the two groups. A nation with low mortality rates – Sweden has been noted as an example – may appear to have large inequalities if the relative method is used.

Other measures present other problems. Measures of illness, whether in the form of symptoms perceived or of judgements about one's own health, offer difficulties of cultural and individual differences, comparability and subjectivity. Statistics of diagnosed disease escape some of this, but are very dependent on perhaps different medical systems for identification. Measures based on function or physical ability raise the question: function for what?

It must be noted that, world-wide, there are considerable differences in perspective. In low-income countries, the extent of poor health among swathes of the population may have very obvious material causes of a lack of services as well as the basic necessities of life. The urgent questions may clearly be the economic and political ones of the extent and distribution of resources. A strong emphasis on equality of access to health care – not the same as equality in health – is also found among some of the wealthiest nations, such as the USA, with largely privatized health systems. Countries with large and disadvantaged ethnic or indigenous groups in their populations may also be particularly concerned with the 'inequality' of the health of different races.

In the UK and most of Western Europe, however, access to health services is relatively universal, and there is a tradition of agreement with the thesis of McKeown that, after a certain stage of economic development has been reached, medical advances and health care do little to explain the improvements in the health of populations in the long run. Inequality in health among their populations has been one of the most prominent concerns in health policy in the UK, Norway, Finland, Sweden, Germany and other European countries, both East and West, ever since the 1970s. In these countries the field of inequality in health has been almost entirely preoccupied with understanding why differences in health by socio-economic status arise, persist, and even grow greater. This preoccupation is less evident in the United States, where a particularly varied population – ethnically and geographically – makes the idea of social class equality in health more complex.

In the UK in particular there has been a tradition of a public health concern about 'unequal' health ever since the mid-nineteenth century, when Chadwick described the living conditions of the poor and showed that defective drainage, unsafe water and overcrowding were inevitably associated with a low expectation of life. In areas such as Bethnal Green

Table 5.1   Life expectancy in Bethnal Green, London, 1842

No. of deaths	Social group	Average age of the deceased
101	Gentlemen and persons engaged in professions, and their families	45 years
273	Tradesmen and their families	26 years
1258	Mechanics, servants and labourers, and their families	16 years

in London, for instance, 'labourers' and their families had life expectancies less than half those of 'gentlemen' (see table 5.1).

Throughout the nineteenth century, life expectancy in all the largest cities of the UK was known to be well below the national average. In inner Liverpool in the 1860s, for instance, it was twenty-five years, ranging from fifteen years for the unemployed and the poor to thirty-five for the more wealthy.

During the industrial revolution, the pioneers of public health focused on the social and physical environment as a primary cause of disease. Concern about inequality within the population remained in the early years of the twentieth century, and was offered as one major justification for the setting up of the National Health Service in 1948, following upon the Beveridge Report of 1942. The 'rediscovery' of inequality was signalled by the setting up and the reporting of the Working Group on Inequalities in Health, the Black Report, in 1980. In the following decades many other nations took up the issue, and the World Health Organization (Europe) issued discussion papers on the concepts and principles of equity in health within nations, and chose the theme as one of those around which its strategy was based (World Health Organization 1998).

The nature and extent of inequalities

We are concerned here with ideas rather than statistics, and the data on 'inequalities' is immense, particularly in the UK, the Nordic countries, and to a lesser extent the other coun-tries of Europe. A few examples will simply show the kind of evidence which is being used and, in particular, the way in which inequality in health is being defined.

In Europe, it has been usual to rely on occupation-based measures of social class or socio-economic status to demon-strate inequality. This type of classification has been used in the UK for almost a century to capture the gradient of status in society, and though it is increasingly seen to have prob-lematic features in modern society, has the advantage of providing continuity for the comparison of statistics.

The original scheme uses the British Registrar General's classification of occupations, and ranges from Social Class I, professional occupations, to Social Class V, unskilled manual occupations. The categorization can be condensed into simple comparisons between 'non-manual' or 'white-collar' occupa-tions' (Social Classes I–IIIa) and 'manual' or 'blue-collar' occupations (Social Classes IIIb–V).

This way of operationalizing 'class' presents difficulties in considering women who are not in the labour force, the unemployed, children, students and the elderly, and in 2001 a new system, the National Statistics Socio-Economic Classification, was adopted in the UK. Many other countries have similar systems, adapted to take account of their occupational structures. In the US, combined scales of income and education have commonly been used.

Socio-economic indicators such as income, education, working status (as distinct from occupation), home-ownership, possession of material goods, or area of residence, which can all be held to be part of the construct of social class, may each be used as independent classifications for demonstrating inequality in health. None, of itself, captures the whole of the relational aspects of class, but each may demonstrate particular relationships. Ethnicity or migrant status are specially important categorizations.

Some typical observations about the extent and nature of inequalities in health follow, simply as examples:

• In the UK, life expectancy at birth is about nine years longer in the 'highest' social class than in the 'lowest'. While the comparison of different nations has many problems (of definitions of social class, or adequacy of data sets), all comparative studies across developed Western nations show the same gradient. Kunst et al. (1998), for instance, compared death rates by class in eleven European countries. The probability of dying between the ages of forty-five and sixty-five for men in manual classes, compared with non-manual classes, was about equally large (five to seven times) in Sweden, Norway, Denmark, England and Wales, Ireland, Italy, Spain and Portugal. Finland and France had the most unfavourable ratios, of 9.8 and 11.5 times respectively.

- Certain regions within countries show consistent health disadvantages over others. Within each region there may be pockets of greater deprivation associated with higher mortality, but for any given level of deprivation the experience of different regions still varies.

- The experience of ill health also varies by social class, though not always as strongly or as regularly as death rates: in one national UK survey, 64 per cent of people over forty years old in manual classes defined their own health as only 'fair' or 'poor', compared with 52 per cent of those in non-manual classes (Cox et al. 1993).

- Everywhere, minority or migrant ethnic groups tend to have higher death rates than the majority population. In the US, the life expectancy of the African-American population in 2007 was 73.3 years, compared to 77.9 years in the White population.

- There are strong and universal differences between men and women: in all countries where there are no longer overwhelming dangers attached to childbirth, women live longer than men. However, they also tend to suffer more illnesses. Since these are to some extent biological differences, how far they can be called 'inequalities' in the sense that has been defined is a matter for debate.

Two aspects of the statistics on inequality have attracted particular attention of recent decades. One is that, measured by social class and by death rates, inequality appears to be increasing. Growing differentials are also apparent for many of the major individual causes of death. There is a need to explain how, in many developed nations, in the virtual absence of absolute deprivation, inequalities in health can persist and even become greater.

The second issue relates to what is known as the 'continuous gradient' or 'fine grain' of inequality. In countries where large proportions of people live in extreme deprivation, or among the poorest minorities which still exist even in developed countries, it is not surprising that health is poorer or life expectancy less. What requires explanation is the fact that the 'threshold model' does not generally hold, that is, that 'inequality' relates only to a level of deprivation below which health is likely to be affected, even in comparatively wealthy societies where most people are likely to be above this level. There is no sharp discontinuity between the minority who lack the basic needs of life, or are exposed to the worst environmental hazards, and the majority whose living conditions meet at least minimum standards. Rather, a straight relationship between socio-economic status and health is found everywhere: health is socially patterned from the bottom to the top of the social scale. This is not a new finding: it has been known ever since national figures of death rates by social class were first produced. Only more recently has it been recognized that it extends – though with perhaps less regularity – to the experience of illness as well as to death rates, that it can be demonstrated to exist throughout the grades of one occupation (the civil service) in the UK (Marmot and Feeney 1996), and that it is an international phenomenon.

One of the most important arguments from the 1970s, strongly related to the changing concept of health, concerned the possible identification of a general susceptibility to ill health related to social class inequalities. The regular pattern of mortality by social class suggests that influences other than polluted environments, dangerous work, smoking and poor diets, which might account for particular forms of ill health, must be involved. It can be suggested that part of the rationale behind the extensive work which identified factors such as stress, lack of control, absence of Antonovsky's salutogenesis, and other psychological explanations involved the search for general causes that might map onto these general patterns. While the effect of specific causes (such as smoking, known to be differentially distributed between social classes) is undoubted, the regular differences in health up and down social scales seemed to be related to generalized differences in susceptibility to disease (Marmot et al. 1984). This work was crucial in turning attention away from single 'unhealthy' behaviours, or a simple emphasis on particular material factors, to a wider concept of social relationships.

However, it has more recently been suggested that attention should return to the patterns of prevalence and death associated with particular diseases. Davey Smith et al. (2001), for instance, reviewing life-course approaches to class inequality, point out that overall statistics of inequality in death rates are strongly influenced by a few important causes of death – CHD, stroke, lung cancer and respiratory disease – which show large socio-economic differences. During the last century, these diseases became the most important and their social gradient became steeper. But different conditions are influenced in different ways – some specially by early-life causes, and some by behaviours or environments in adulthood. These are diseases which usually show themselves only after relatively long exposure to risk factors, and the social gradients are due to the social circumstances within which lives are played out. Looking at specific diseases can contribute to more complex and satisfactory models of what we mean by social class inequality in health.

The causes of inequality

These discussions lead to the main issue of debate: the cause of inequality in health, especially the causes of the apparent increase in inequality in the Western world. In the individual, how, exactly, do social inequalities affect health and how do patterns of health inequality develop over the life-course? What are the mechanisms by which the health of populations is related to structural features of societies? The answer to these questions are essential for policy-makers who wish to reduce inequalities, and at the same time they are part of the story about how health is defined in contemporary Western society.

The Black Report in the UK in 1980 discussed three types of explanation of 'real' inequalities, if the demonstrated social class differences were not simply artefacts of statistics and the changing composition of social classes over time. It was shown that in fact, although there were indeed problems of measurement, they did not change the broad picture or make inequality 'disappear'. The three remaining types of explanation were those relating to natural and social selection involving health-related mobility; explanations relating to the lifestyles and health-related habits of different groups in society; and materialist or structural explanations which focus on the direct effects of living and working conditions. Macintyre (1997) pointed out that for each of these there is a 'hard' and a 'soft' version. The 'hard' version is that a favoured type of explanation is the only cause of (or explains away) social variation in health. The 'soft' version, on the other hand, recognizes that the types of explanation are not exclusive, and each makes a contribution. She noted that the Black Report, while seeing material factors as the most important, and rejecting the 'hard' versions of the other explanations, did not suggest that these 'soft' versions were untrue or irrelevant. Some of the debate of the 1980s which followed the Black Report took up unhelpfully polarized positions, concentrating attacks on the 'hard' versions of explanation: this seemed to be necessary in a political climate in the UK where it was felt important to stress the material causes of increasing inequality.

In the last few decades a more productive, though inevitably more complicated and difficult, effort has been made to explore the interrelation between and contribution of different types of explanation. Life-course studies are showing that selection by health certainly takes place, with the healthy moving up the social scale and the unhealthy suffering occupational disadvantage, but this does not explain away inequality as no more than the inevitable consequence of this social sorting. The concept of health capital, introduced in chapter 3, is relevant. Cohort studies which follow populations from the day of their birth demonstrate its utility. Wadsworth (1991), for instance, has shown, in relation to a British cohort born in 1946, how health capital accumulates or is dispersed. A poor start in life, associated with poorer parental socio-economic circumstances and vulnerability to illness, can be reinforced throughout childhood by poorer education and thus lower social class in adulthood, less healthy behaviour, and poorer health. The 'imprint of time' takes place over the individual life-course but also depends on historical time: as the social environment changes, each cohort has a unique health history. Concepts of the cause of health and disease move beyond simple cause and effect to become more complex and more individual.

Simple models which stress only the importance of behavioural patterns and voluntarily chosen lifestyles (with health education as the obvious remedy) have to allow for the fact that lifestyles depend on social relationships and histories and the cultures of areas and groups. Poverty, in a society with high inequality, is associated with neighbourhoods and living conditions which make healthy living more difficult. Interventions designed to improve health may even widen social disparities, for instance, in the case of screening programmes or health education taken up more readily by the more advantaged. Bourdieu's key concept of habitus, explaining how routine practices are influenced by the external structure of individuals' social worlds and in turn reproduce this structure (discussed in chapter 4), is also relevant. Physical capital, Bourdieu argued, develops in conjunction with social forces and is integral to the maintenance of social inequality.

The materialist explanations have been given weight by the wealth of evidence that inequality in health is directly associated with income, occupational status and disadvantaged areas. Even here, however, 'hard' versions have to be tempered by consideration of relative, rather than absolute, poverty, and the consideration of psychosocial mechanisms as well as direct physical effects. Social inequalities affect how people perceive the world and themselves. Less equal societies are simply less healthy environments.

The socio-biologic translation

The phenomenon of increasing inequality, and the pattern of a regular gradient up and down the social scale, require explanations in biological terms. Dysfunction, disease and death must have actual physiological causes. Throughout life, it is easy to see how the most obvious insults in a less advantaged life – pollution, diet, hygiene, accidents, harmful work, poor housing – harm health, but it is difficult to see them as more than a partial explanation for gradients throughout the social scale.

It is agreed that the mechanisms are not, largely, genetic. For instance, it has been estimated that straightforward genetic inheritance may account for between only 1 and 5 per cent of the total disease burden, and indirect evidence such as blood grouping shows that social classes are genetically mixed, not homogeneous. Events associated typically with mothers in poor circumstances which occur at or before birth are certainly demonstrated to cast life-long shadows in terms of poor or 'unequal' health, but again they are only a partial explanation. Inequality in health grows greater as individuals grow older.

Thus a need is felt for what Tarlov (1996: 71) called the socio-biologic translation: the way in which social characteristics are perceived, processed into biological signals, and converted into actual disease. It has long been known that distress, grief and other damaging emotions can harm physical health: this is part of the social model. That psychological stress can also contribute to mental illness, or effect health-damaging behaviour, is obvious, but the search has been for specific biological mechanisms by which it can be transformed into specific diseases or into general susceptibility. The biological systems known to be concerned are common to most mammals: on perceiving threat or danger, the body is prepared for flight or fight through the endocrine and nervous systems, and adverse consequences for health result if arousal is sustained or constantly recurring.

The concepts which are invoked to provide the link to social circumstances are those such as feelings of control, self-efficacy and social cohesion. Low social status engenders psychological distress which is expressed in feelings such as shame, lack of self-esteem, and lack of dignity and respect. It is known within psychology that insecurity and the disturbed family functioning that may arise in adverse social situations in early childhood makes people more vulnerable in adulthood. Children brought up with different experiences of attachment and conflict use different strategies to cope with the stresses of threatening environments. Stressors, particularly those which are long-term, are unevenly distributed in society, to a large extent cumulative and parallel with material resources. Practical coping and buffering resources – education, access to help, useful networks – which might help to alleviate the effects of stress are similarly differentially distributed by social class. Thus biological science, psychology and sociology come together to flesh out the possible mechanisms of the socio-biologic translation

This area of research and discussion about health inequality at the level of individuals within any given society is raised to the level of explaining the health of societies by the work of Richard Wilkinson and others. Wilkinson (1996) noted that, even though the health differences within societies are closely related to socio-economic status, once a country has reached a certain state of economic development, the population can be, as a whole, more than twice as rich as another country without being healthier:

> Despite the strong relationships between income and health that have been found repeatedly within countries, when you look at differences between the rich developed countries, you find – at best – only a weak relationship between their average incomes and their standards of health. For instance, even after allowing for price differences, Greeks have less than half the average income of Americans and yet are healthier. Similarly, although life expectancy in most developed countries tends to increase by two or three years every decade, this improvement it not closely related to economic growth: one country's economy can grow twice as fast as another's for perhaps twenty years and yet its citizens may not benefit from any additional growth in life expectancy. Income differences appear to be important within rich countries, but not between them. Even among the fifty states of the USA, where cultural differences are smaller than those between countries, there is (after allowing for differences in income distribution) no relationship between mortality and average state income. Yet within each state there is a clear link between income and health. (Wilkinson 2000: 10)

Wilkinson suggested that the most plausible explanation was that what matters to health, after a certain stage of development has been reached, is relative income and social status, not absolute income. The extent of social inequalities within nations is both a cause and an indicator of the health differences between nations. This relates not only to income inequality, but also to inequality in power and status. The greater the inequality in a society, manifested by authoritative power patterns and undemocratic institutions, as well as by a particularly unequal distribution of income and wealth, the poorer the health of that society. Material inequality engenders social divisions, which result in anxiety, conflict and other negative emotions, from which health status suffers. The mechanisms of the association can also be indirect, through behaviours ranging from alcohol and tobacco use to violent crime or the prevalence of firearm use. Countries with less social inequality, in contrast, tend to have more security, social support, trust and self-respect, all conducive to better health.

This thesis is supported by many studies which show that more equal countries, with smaller income differences between rich and poor, tend to have better health statistics, as measured not only by surveys of self-assessed health but also by mortality rates. Among the developed countries, there is a tendency for the most egalitarian, not necessarily the richest, to have the highest life expectancy. Wilkinson suggests, for instance, that Japan, which by the end of the 1980s had become the country with the highest life expectancy in the world, seemed a highly cohesive society, with a long period of narrowing income differences and, uniquely in the developed world, falling crime rates. The relationship between income inequality and death rates has been shown both at the level of regions within countries and as comparisons between countries. As Wilkinson noted, this applies, for instance, in the fifty states of the USA, independently of average incomes, or the proportion of the population in absolute poverty, or expenditure on medical care.

Neo-materialist explanations

Other commentators have put forward a slightly different explanation for the relationship between health and income distribution within societies, criticizing too great an emphasis on psychosocial processes, and considering a broader set of social determinants of health. For instance, Coburn (2000) suggests that the psychosocial effects of perceived relative deprivation are less important than the fact that in more equal societies a wide range of factors, including public services, are more likely to be available to the whole population. The more market-oriented or neo-liberal the regime, the greater the inequalities and the more the social fragmentation. Economic globalization and competition associated with the international spread of neo-liberalism increase income, but they are also a cause of greater economic inequality, poorer cohesion, and more inequality in health. The effect of economic inequality may depend on the availability of public services. In unequal societies, such things as housing, health care or education may present problems for those who are relatively poor. This is suggested as a more important difference than the perception of social hierarchies.

The variation between countries with different welfare regimes has been analysed in various ways. In Europe, though considerable inequalities in morbidity and mortality are present across the continent, evidence varies about the relationship of inequalities and organization of social benefits. Clusters of welfare regimes can be constructed, and their apparent effects considered: for instance, the welfare systems common in family-oriented Southern European countries do not seem to buffer ill health among disadvantaged groups. On the other hand, the distribution of welfare benefits within social democratic Scandanavian countries appears to have a protective effect for the disadvantaged.

Social capital

These types of explanation, to the extent that they emphasize the concept of social cohesion, are to some extent a return to Durkheim, and the demonstration that 'social facts' are more than the sum of individuals and that social health is related to social norms and social solidarity. The relevant concept of 'social capital' has, for several decades, driven one of the most active fields of discussion and research about the relationship of society and health. It is proposed as a way of explaining how community-level influences impinge on health, and embraces all the social, economic and cultural resources to which a population or group has access. For instance, studies comparing the different states of the USA have found that mortality rates are associated with levels of social capital, even adjusting for individual risk factors in the population such as low income or education, lack of access to health care, or the prevalence of unhealthy behaviours.

Essentially, social capital can be a version of communitarianism: it originates in community networks and voluntary organizations, because these settings provide potential for cooperative action and social support. Social connectedness or cohesion is generated by networks: this is what holds communities together and enables them to act for the common benefit.

The best-known proponent is the political scientist Robert Putnam, who credited Coleman with first having developed the theoretical framework. Coleman (1988) had defined the concept as not a single entity but a variety of different entities, with two elements in common. They all consist of some aspect of social structures, within which they facilitate certain actions of persons or corporate actors. Like other forms of capital, social capital is productive, making possible the achievement of various ends. It was essentially a property of communities, not individuals: 'It is not lodged either in the actors themselves or in physical implements of production.' It is thus distinct from the concept of 'health capital', discussed in chapter 3, though the social capital of communities may include their health capital as one component.

Putnam (1995: 67) used the idea of social capital to explain the findings from a twenty-year study of regional government in Italy. He suggested that,

> For a variety of reasons, life is easier in communities blessed with a substantial stock of social capital. In the first place, networks of civic engagement foster sturdy norms of generalized reciprocity and encourage the emergence of social trust. Such networks facilitate coordination and communication, amplify reputations, and thus allow dilemmas of collective

action to be resolved . . . At the same time, networks of civic engagement embody past success at collaboration, which can serve as a cultural template for future collaboration. Finally, dense networks of interaction probably broaden the participants' sense of self, developing 'I' into the 'we', or . . . enhancing the participants' 'taste' for collective benefits.

In research, various approaches and definitions of the concept have been used. Four may be distinguished:

- Coleman's definition of social capital as the structures of relationships in society, involving norms, obligations, relationships, sanctions, and access to resources
- Putnam's description as features of social organization such as norms, networks and social trust that facilitate coordination and cooperation for mutual benefit
- Bourdieu's more specific definition: the aggregate of resources, linked to membership of groups, which provide collectively owned capital
- Portez's application of the idea more clearly to individuals, defining social capital as the ability of actors to secure benefits by virtue of membership in social networks or other social structures.

The definition most commonly used is that of Putnam, and the key constructs within the concept are social relationships and networks, group affiliation and civic activity. Trust, developed through norms of reciprocity or mutual help, and networks of engagement in public affairs, are crucial. The research which attempts to test the concept tries to measure such things as social support, reciprocity, neighbourliness and feelings of belonging, activity in local groups (including religious groups), trust both in the people around and in local institutions, self-perceived control, power and influence over decisions, and feelings of exclusion or inclusion in the community. These are the things which come to define community 'health'.

They are necessarily usually 'measured' at the individual level by asking questions of people, and the answers aggregated to represent the community, but societal-level characteristics can also be used to represent what has been called the embeddedness or autonomy of groups. Statistics such as overall voting levels can be used as a measure of civic participation. There are also attempts to find indicators which can in some sense stand in for social cohesion, trust and reciprocity. For instance, it has been found that crime statistics, in the USA, and even such a simple measure as levels of gun ownership (which is of course correlated with crime and violence), are associated at geographical levels with income inequality (with average level of income taken into account). It is suggested that what is being identified is normative structures which encourage or inhibit crime, and this says something about social cohesion.

Some critical views have been raised about these models (Foley and Edwards 1999). It has been suggested that, in the studies finding associations between income inequality and population mortality, there are conceptual difficulties in using aggregate cross-sectional data as a means of testing hypotheses about the effect of income and its distribution on the health of individuals. Any focus on current incomes may in any case be too crude an indicator of accumulated health influences over life-times. Social capital theory has been criticized because of some ambiguity about the meaning and definition in practice of 'community', because the actual measures of 'commitment' or 'engagement' are held to be too oriented to middle-class values, and because close networks can be oppressive rather than supportive, or – in the example of, for instance, drug-using communities – health-harming rather than health-enhancing. Kunitz (2001: 170) notes that the quest for community ('certainly in the US, perhaps the most individualistic of nations') does not invariably lead to improved health, 'for social ties may bind us together, but they may also imprison us'.

Social capital is an attractive model, bringing together the tradition of research on 'stress' in the social model of health and the socio-biologic translation, with explanations for population health, in ways appealing to policy-makers. Muntaner et al. (2000: 107) described social capital as

an alternative to the structural inequalities of class, gender, race, by bringing to the forefront of social epidemiology an appealing common-sense social philosophy to which everyone can relate, that is, good relations with your community are good for your health.

But it is argued that the concept neglects the distributive dimension, the way in which different societies distribute power and resources, economically and politically. The concept gives great importance to voluntary organizations and community groups, but the extent to which these have any influence or potential to contribute must depend on particular systems of checks and balances, ways of administration – in other words, their relationship, in a given country, to the state. Different linkages have different degrees of significance, and may – especially those likely to make up the networks of the less privileged – have no power at all, or, like the trades unions, have less than they did.

Kunitz (2001) points to the roots of the idea of social capital in the nineteenth century, originally in the work of Durkheim and de Tocqueville, who were responding to the political pressures of their own time: 'but our world is different from theirs'. At the level of individual health, he illustrates

> some of the ways in which the larger context may influence the structure, functions, and effectiveness of social networks, and how they may in turn influence various dimensions of people's health and use of services. That is to say, social relations are not always supportive and may be damaging. This is particularly so when poverty, unemployment, insecurity and inadequate infrastructure of formal organization are prevalent. (Kunitz 2001: 167)

Considering particularly the application of the concept in the USA, he points to the legacy of civic cultures implanted in the North and the South as relevant to the higher social capital and lower mortality in the North. For the inequalities of metropolitan areas and the industrial heartland, the social history of the late nineteenth and early twentieth centuries must be invoked. The history and structure of specific populations and places are related both to social networks and to health. Qualitative work on social capital in the UK has also shown clearly (Swann and Morgan 2002) that the networks, social engagement, trust, reciprocity and cohesion which make up the currency of social capital research have to be linked with local cultures, social histories and policy environments. Since socio-political settings are so relevant, social capital must take different forms in different countries, and cannot be expected to be the same everywhere.

Discussion continues, but these ways of looking at health remain perhaps the most interesting contemporary ideas about health and society. In particular, they draw attention to the importance of considering health in positive terms – asking what affects the body's defences – rather than simply in negative terms as exposure to external material hazards. They lead, finally, to some consideration of the postmodern view of health, and where ideas about health are currently moving.

Further reading

Blane, D., Brunner, E. and Wilkinson, R. 1996: *Health and Social Organisation*. London: Routledge.

Heyman, J., Herzman, C. B., Currer, L. B. and Evans, R. G. (eds) 2006: *Healthier Societies: From Analysis to Action*. Oxford: Oxford University Press.

Leon, D. and Walt, G. (eds) 2001: *Poverty, Inequality and Health*. Oxford: Oxford University Press.

McKeown, T. 1976: *The Role of Medicine: Dream, Mirage or Nemesis?* London: Nuffield Provincial Hospitals Trust.

Marmot, M. 2004: *Status Syndrome: How Your Social Standing Directly Affects Your Health and Life Expectancy*. London: Bloomsbury.

Navarro, V. (ed.) 2007: *Neoliberalism, Globalisation and Inequalities – Consequences for Health and Quality of Life*. Amityville, NY: Baywood Pub.

Wilkinson, R. 1996: *Unhealthy Societies: The Afflictions of Inequality*. London: Routledge.

6

Contemporary Change in the Meaning of Health

We live, of course, in a time of explosive change and development in medical science and technology. New knowledge and new techniques offer longer life and more control over our bodies, at least in those societies wealthy enough to afford them. At the same time there are new problems – the resurgence of tuberculosis, the appearance of antibiotic-resistant bacteria, the long struggle to control HIV/AIDS, unexpected diseases such as New Variant CJD or the new respiratory viruses spreading world-wide during the early twenty-first century – and some perception among the public that 'modern living' creates its own illnesses, so that the sick person wonders:

> Are we dealing with an illness of the individual or with an illness of society? Is cancer part of myself, or does it come to me from the outside world? (Herzlich and Pierret 1987: 65)

The theme of this chapter is not the overambitious one of predicting where the art and science of medicine may be going, or what achievements there may be in the future. Rather, it is to examine these contemporary trends in order to speculate on whether they are causing changes in fundamental definitions of health and illness. First, it is suggested that technology, in the condition called postmodernity, changes boundaries between the self and the body. Secondly, there are changing boundaries between ill and not-ill, largely as an effect of the 'new genetics', where screening introduces new ideas of disease-in-waiting and new discourses of health. Thirdly, modern technologies have been accused of taking over both birth and the end of life, changing fundamental boundaries between life and death. Fourthly, the distinction between self and not-self, or the body and not-body, is blurred by developments such as the replacement of body parts, organ donation, and stem cell technology. The use of technologies for 'enhancement' rather than for therapy again raises questions about the boundaries of disease and patienthood.

Technology and postmodernity

These trends refer to the most obvious definition of technology as scientific developments, machines and new procedures. These may be considered as neutral artifacts, simply means of delivering care. But it has been argued that they are never in fact neutral: they shape the way in which bodies and disorders are defined and experienced (Berg and Mol 1998). They should be regarded as active transformers not only of health care, but actually of health itself. Moreover, in recent decades the term technology has (sometimes confusingly) assumed a wider meaning in health studies: not only devices, manufactured artifacts or even drugs or forms of treatment, but closer to Foucault's 'technologies of power', in which organized forms of social and institutional action are all regarded as technologies.

Three general approaches to technology are described in a review by Timmermans and Berg (2003). First, *techonological determinism* sees technology as a driving force, with innovation shaped by technical variables alone. Secondly, *social essentialism* sees technology as a blank slate, rendered meaningful and given shape only through social interaction and interpretation, and influenced by interest groups who are in a position to select certain innovations over others. Thirdly, *technology in practice* is suggested as a more complex approach which includes consideration of governments' health policies, the variety of expert knowledge claims, the normative dynamics of decision-making, and the embededness of technologies with other practices, tools and social groups.

In this wider sense, technology is defined, to quote Lehoux (2006: 45), as all the things that 'structure the delivery, organization and outcome of health care'. These enter into values and beliefs, as well as the practical experience of health-care systems. Information systems, protocols and bases of evidence all become part of technology. The 'multiple realities' of medical records become a technology of themselves, blurring the single, whole, identity of the patient (Berg and Bowker 1997). These 'soft' technologies also have the potential for changing the definition of illness and the patient, and generate effects on identity and selfhood.

This creates a world which is

> . . . a complex, fragmented and paradoxical one. Its boundaries and contours are difficult to delineate, its societal participants not always obvious or easy to discern, its rules of engagement variable and contested, information about it relatively difficult to obtain, its terminologies multiple and independent, its technology classifications labyrinthine and bureaucratic. (Faulkner 2009: 27)

For many theorists, these new technologies, both hard and soft, are the hallmark of postmodernity, high modernity, or the late modern period in contemporary advanced industrial societies. These are differently defined by various commentators, but in general they replace the modernity which was defined as characterized by stability, security, the clear work patterns and stable hierarchies of manufacturing industry, and confidence in the advance of science (and thus confidence in medicine and doctors). Postmodernity is a period of segmented markets and a more complex and fragmented social structure. Industrial jobs are replaced by work in communications and services, work becomes more flexible, and job insecurity rises. Corporate capitalism and consumer lifestyles shaped by popular culture are dominant. The period is characterized by the rise of transnational companies and the expansion of the global economy. Change has become more common, social relations are in a state of flux, and life is more reflexive. Individuals are separated from their traditional ties and become linked, rather, by market relations. Identity is constructed around social practices and cultural consumption, and rather than being determined by the traditional categories of class, gender, age, race and so on becomes fluid and self-directed. Shilling (1993: 3) points to a contemporary paradox:

> We now have the means to exert an unprecedented degree of control over bodies, yet we are also living in an age which has thrown into radical doubt our knowledge of what bodies are and how we should control them.

As a result of technology, the body is increasingly becoming a phenomenon of options and choices.

In this society characterized by change, choice and adaptability, a sense of self is no longer 'given'. Elliott (2001: 136) described the three states of mind that define the core contours of postmodern selfhood:

> Firstly, there is an emphasis upon fragmentation. The postmodernist critique suggests that the contemporary self is so fragmented, multiple and dispersed that the symbolic consistency and narrative texture of experience disintegrates. In a world invaded by new technologies and saturated with flashy commodities, the self loses its consistency, and becomes brittle, broken or shattered. Secondly, the flickering media surfaces of postmodern culture are, according to this view, mirrored internally, so that a narcissistic preoccupation with appearance, image and style dominates the regulation of the self. Thirdly, there is a new centrality accorded to fantasy and phantasmagoria on the personal and social levels, so that the dream, hallucination and madness take on an added importance at the expense of common stocks of knowledge or rationality. In conditions of postmodernity, in the West at any rate, people seem to be experiencing a mixture of confusion, dispersal and disillusionment on the one hand, and excitement, desire and the possibility for personal development on the other.

In medicine, it has been suggested that technologies – from X-rays to computer tomography, magnetic resonance imaging, or CAT scans – privilege the 'image' over the actual body and its experiences. Baudrillard had argued that the movement into the high-tech postmodern world meant entrance into hyperreality. Imaging and visualization become central, the distinction between what is represented and its representation disappears, and simulations come to constitute 'reality'. In the wider society, the production of goods is replaced by the production of models and simulations, and the real and the image become difficult to distinguish. Machines replace the patient, and, to a degree, the doctor.

Changing boundaries between ill and not-ill

A second effect of technological change is that the boundaries of illness become blurred. The 'surveillance society' described in chapter 5 rests on technological developments. It requires not only ever more sophisticated measures and instruments, but also an administrative apparatus that can survey and screen populations. Essentially, it is identifying 'normality'. Any sharp divisions between healthy and not-healthy are replaced by a continuum: there is 'normal' variation, and even to be outside it is not necessarily 'ill', but may be potentially ill. Medicine targets everyone, not just those diagnosed as diseased, and everyone is to some degree at risk: as Armstrong (1995: 400) notes, it is

> a world in which everything is normal and at the same time precariously abnormal, and in which a future that can be transformed remains a constant possibility.

The 'remission society' described by Frank (chapter 1) is also relevant. People are not only potentially ill, but ill-in-remission, or ill but technologically returned to (functional) 'normality' by prostheses, pacemakers, transplants, and mechanical body regulators of many kinds. The triumph of modern medicine is that so many people have their lives prolonged by these means. The problem is that people are left 'needing a new map for their lives' (Frank 1995: 10).

As knowledge about disease and its measurable, though not necessarily experienced, precursors increases, and a battery of tests – blood tests, amniocentesis, genetic screening – become possible, new diseases-in-waiting are created. Techniques of diagnosis – mammography, screening for prostate cancer – make it possible to identify potential problems. They also, however, can give rise to anxieties, since the tests may be indeterminate or give results only in terms of relative risks. The knowledge of these may offer difficult choices, such as prophylactic surgical removal of the breasts or prostate. It is not easy to make rational decisions about these, since the risks are rarely precise. Acting and not acting both have costs. Thus there are debates about breast cancer screening – undoubtedly lifesaving for some, but traumatic (because of false negative and false positive results) for many. The PSA test for prostate cancer has similarly been criticized for 'swamping' services by diagnosing conditions which may not pose an immediate health risk (Faulkner 2009: 74). Two-thirds of men undergoing biopsy after the results of this test are said not to have cancer. People who are HIV-positive are, again, an example of the potentially but not yet ill. Thus, the discussion of HIV testing in the 1980s – before better therapies for prolonging life with HIV became available, so that tests had definite advantages for the individual – raised in stark form the disadvantages, both social and psychological, of choosing to enter the disease-in-waiting state, and the tension between these and the necessity to promote testing for public health purposes.

Mechanic (2002: 459) suggested that screening and prevention are not only technologically driven but shaped by contemporary values – market competition, faith in modern technical progress, activism and consumerism. They may 'take patients on treatment trajectories that are difficult to control and which result in being labelled with diagnoses they do not have and receiving interventions they do not need'. The 'gift of knowing' (Kenen 1996: 1547) is a questionable gift:

Technology is Circe – handmaiden of the medical profession. The media, some health care professionals and informal kinship and friendship networks bombard individuals (mainly those with comprehensive health insurance) with messages about the value of recent biotechnical breakthroughs.

The growing development of 'home test' kits is widely thought to present dangers, since the results can be misinterpreted or can seriously affect 'patients', despite any warnings the manufacturers may issue. Cases such as the PSA test for prostate cancer are extreme, but the same applies to less dramatic conditions and more routine tests, performed out of administrative habit (or sometimes out of commercial pressures), or simply because they are possible. Examples include commercially available self-operated blood pressure monitors, or coagulometers which monitor the viscosity of the blood. The latter are widely prescribed so that those using anticoagulants for e.g. thrombosis or heart disease may manage their own regime.

A trend towards ever more self- and professional monitoring is driven by various pressures. The possibility of missing life-threatening diagnoses will always be important to practitioners; governments are concerned to present themselves as fostering preventive public health; private medical screening companies, often insurance-funded, proliferate. The movement towards screening becomes allied to pressures towards self-responsibility and self-care, and the empowerment of the patient.

In a medical model, 'at risk' and 'abnormal' become confused. Similarly, in lay discourse, 'proneness' to illness consists of a mixture of ideas about heredity, immune status, individual make-up, and the consequences of health history: 'She's not one to take colds'; 'All the family are prone to arthritis'; 'I've been liable to depression ever since that event'; 'I'm healthy but prone to migraine.'

The new genetics

This confusion is especially fostered by the 'new genetics', that is, the body of knowledge and practice based on recombinant DNA technology, exemplified by the Human Genome Project, the great international enterprise which was directed

towards mapping out the whole of the human genetic structure. This technology may present many future problems
associated with the possibility of predicting health risks based
on genetic make-up. Causes of disquiet include insurance
issues, the dangers of discrimination, and confusion about
what disablement means. It is also argued that genetics
becomes privileged over other factors which influence health.

Genetic screening is already common (at least in the USA)
in industries such as chemicals, electronics, oil and pharmaceuticals, to identify those who may be 'genetically susceptible'. Again, there are opposing movements: that towards
social responsibility, and that towards individuals' rights to
privacy and ownership of the information contained in their
own body.

Meanwhile, genetic testing for disease involves two groups
of conditions. In late-onset dominant conditions, the inheritance of a single copy of a gene puts the individual at risk of
developing disease. Genetic markers for Huntingdon's
Disease, for instance, have been available since the mid 1980s.
Hereditary breast and ovarian cancer are other conditions for
which testing programmes are available, and predictive
testing at any time throughout life can gauge the likelihood
of developing the disease. On the other hand, there are recessive conditions where individuals who inherit a faulty gene
from both parents will inevitably develop the condition
(examples include cystic fibrosis or Tay–Sachs Disease) at
birth or early in life. Those who inherit a single copy will be
carriers, who will not have the disease themselves but will
pass it on to, on average, half their offspring.

Each of these presents difficult, but different, problems
associated with the definition of health. The foetus may be
tested, raising the possibility of avoiding the birth of potentially unhealthy children through abortion. In some cultures
and from some ethical positions the 'selection' of healthy
babies in this way is unacceptable. Predictive testing for late-
onset conditions provides the opportunity to 'know' one's
fate, but there are psychological and emotional difficulties in
receiving this information if therapy is not available. Those
diagnosed as having an increased possibility – or even the
certainty – of developing disease may spend a lifetime as what
Kenen (1994) called PPDs (Possible Potentially Diseased) or

DIWs (Diseased in Waiting) with all the probable distress or discrimination that this entails. These issues are stark in a single gene disorder such as Huntingdon's, where disease is, at present, inevitable in an individual who lives long enough. On the other hand, unless those at risk of late-onset disease, or carrying recessive conditions, are tested, they may pass disease on to their children unknowingly. There are added complications if only some forms of a disease are related to a specific gene: it is thought, for instance, that this applies to only 3 to 5 per cent of cases of ovarian cancer.

When a disease is defined as genetic it moves from being an individual issue to being a family disease. Genetic risk becomes even more clearly a moral issue: in a study in the UK of women attending genetic counselling for hereditary breast/ovarian cancer, they

> perceive themselves as having a responsibility to their kin (past, present and future generations) to establish the magnitude of their risk and the risk to other family members, and to act on this information by engaging in some form of risk management. (Hallowell 1999: 597)

To pass on a gene, Hallowell notes, is not 'fault', but it is certainly 'a kind of responsibility'. Many studies have demonstrated the way in which families construct the meaning of hereditary risk within their everyday lives and how in turn these constructions shape the experience of predictive testing. Michie et al. (1996), for instance, described the role of 'functional pessimism' and 'uncertain wellness' in the case of the familial disease adenomatous polyposis. Cox and McKellin (1999) discussed how, in the case of Huntingdon's Disease, families adapted and modified their understanding of scientific risk, jointly engaging in a fluid and contingent 'social calculus of risk'.

Where prophylactic measures are available, as for breast and ovarian cancer, screening may be made available and used by those who believe, from their family history, that they are susceptible or 'prone' to the disease. Research has shown how prophylactic surgery can be seen by patients as both securing and undermining their present and future self-identities. Failure to take advantage of screening, not 'wanting to know', can be seen as morally irresponsible. However, if screening suggests action then this produces competing risks. In the case of ovarian cancer, Hallowell and Lawton (2002) described women's dilemmas in terms of maintaining or losing fertility, and maintaining or losing femininity, rather than ideas of 'illness', with the women saying, for instance: 'That's part of you being taken away, really, that's part of your role on earth being removed' (p. 434); 'ageing before your time', or 'for potential risk when I'm 80, I've wrecked my life now' (p. 437).

It is commonly suggested that the new genetics not only creates these ill/not-ill dilemmas for the individual, but is affecting the whole discourse of health and illness. The gene is becoming an icon, perhaps especially in American society, and a kind of genetic fatalism – assuming that genetic make-up determines a wide range of behaviour and 'innate' characteristics – underlies much public discourse. Conrad (1999) notes that genetic explanations are readily accepted by the public, even in cases where the evidence is limited, and there is a sense in which popular views of genetics look backwards in terms of concepts of health. The model is of specific etiology, where one gene or genetic mutation can cause a disease or behaviour – the 'breast cancer gene', the 'obesity gene' – in what is called the OGOD (one gene, one disease) concept, with complex interactions and contextual effects ignored. Conrad suggests this shows parallels with the acceptance of germ theory in the early twentieth century, and is accepted because it resonates with it. At the same time it appeals to current Western ideas of individualism and self-responsibility, 'a form of genetic determinism that assumes (in language at least) that there are specific genes for specific traits under all circumstances'. In fact:

> Virtually everyone has some genes that make them susceptible to diseases or traits we might find problematic. All of us are genetically liable to some human trouble, be it allergies, near-sightedness, baldness, depression, or forms of heart disease or cancer. The trick is to understand how these susceptibilities interact with particular environments to produce human traits or disorders. (Conrad 1999: 238)

At the same time, the 'geneticization' of society can imply that health becomes de-individualized. Health becomes a family issue: to assess an individual's risk may involve their kin, and people become involved in complex networks of health (Wertz 1992). Genetic 'risk' becomes identified not in the specific body but in computer programmes of 'pedigrees' or family histories.

There are obvious concerns about where the new genetics may be taking medicine. The increasing use of DNA databases threatens what Nelkin and Andrews (1999) call 'surveillance creep', a controlling tool for organizations and governments. The role of corporate industry also becomes increasingly important, not only in shaping the therapy of gene technology but also in choosing the direction of research.

An example is the new specialities of *pharmacogenetics* and *pharmacogenomics*, or the study of the genetic variation underlying the different responses that patients may have to drugs, which have expanded rapidly with the completion of the Human Genome Project and the development of technologies which enable cheap genetic testing. The combination of pharmacological and genetic or genomic knowledge to predict drug reactions offers the prospect of tailoring pharmaceutical drugs not just to the disease, but actually to the individual. The aim is to enter a new era of tailor-made medicines, avoiding side-effects and adverse reactions. Obviously, there are pressures on the pharmaceutical industry to identify the best drug doses and the patients who are going to be more or less responsive, and there are pressures on health providers to supply drugs efficiently and reduce costs. There is no certainty that this can be achieved, and questions are raised, in any case, about the proliferation of genetic testing which is implied, and the inevitable 'politics' of personalized medicine. One international study of the views of patients diagnosed with depression about genome-based drugs (Barr and Rose 2009), for instance, showed considerable ambivalence about these therapies, and how their clinical acceptability was bound up with models of disease and the relationship of illness and self-hood.

Genetic screening produces not only new states in between health and illness for the individual, but also these wider new ways of thinking about disease and disability. Various types of genetic choice, from sex selection to personality traits, theoretically become available through new reproductive technologies, cloning, or gene therapy. Disability activists worry that genetic interventions will inevitably lead to a new form of eugenics, with a diminished value placed on people with disabilities. Now that the idea of genetic disease has been extended from single-gene inherited disease to many conditions such as heart disease, the possibility of gene therapy for a broad range of common acquired conditions tends to reconceptualize all illness within the language of molecular genetics. As Novas and Rose (2000: 485) suggested,

> The rise of the person genetically at risk is one aspect of a wider change in the vision of life itself – a new 'molecular optics'. Life is now imagined, investigated, explained, and intervened upon at a molecular level – in terms of the molecular structure of bodily components, the molecular processes of life functions, and the molecular properties of pharmaceutical products.

Meanwhile, new technologies – including also the fields of organ transplantation and intensive care – are already raising ethical questions about the distribution of health resources. The issues raise concerns not only about who is ill, and what is disease, but also about who will be – inevitably – selected for 'treatment' and who will not.

Changing boundaries of life and death

It is not only the boundary between health and illness which is blurring, but the most fundamental boundary of all – that distinguishing life from not-life. This is particularly true at the beginning and the end of life.

At the beginning, developments in reproductive technology call into question when a new life commences. The identification of the precise moment is probably not something that can be assessed scientifically. Is it at fertilization? At implantation? At a certain stage of foetal development? Not until living apart from the mother? Technologies for the treatment of disease or damage to the foetus move personhood or patienthood back before birth. Perhaps the extreme example of this is foetal surgery to the the 'unborn patient', where the foetus is partially removed from a pregnant woman's uterus, operated upon, and replaced within the mother's body for further development.

Fundamental decisions have to be made about the start of life especially in the context of contraception and abortion. Technologies associated with reproductive genetics present choices which are associated with the actual creation of life, with profound social consequences. Technologies such as IVF and surrogate motherhood raise questions not only about fertility, but also about the definition of the family, and about the meaning of motherhood and fatherhood. Administrative and legal definitions have to be made about who, in what circumstances, is a mother, about the difference between a biological and a social father, and about who, under what circumstances, has what rights and obligations. New social roles are created, such as sperm donor or surrogate mother. Manipulation of eggs, sperm and embryos outside the body offers moral dilemmas: prenatal diagnosis or gene therapy for serious disease is generally acceptable, but 'designer babies' are not. Similarly, help for infertility is to be welcomed, but the turning of babies into commodities condemned.

Modern technological medicine has been accused of taking over both birth and death, and transferring them from the category of a normal part of 'healthy' lives to the medicalized realm of the pathological. It has been argued that the advent of hospital medicine was largely responsible for the handing over of birth and death to specialists and their removal from the public view. Death, in particular, became hidden, avoided, verging on the obscene. Commentators such as Aries noted how modern Western societies tended to deny death, seeing it as the enemy, often 'untimely', and a failure of medicine – almost an 'unnatural' event. The 'good' death, peaceful and accepting, is presented as an ideal, but an ideal that few are permitted to experience. At the same time, the wish for individual control which is held to be characteristic of late modern societies is now responsible for a desire to control one's own dying, as one's own childbearing, rather than hand it over to the system of medicine. Thus there is some shift (though not necessarily in all cultures) to hospice and palliative care for the dying, and rising support for the right to make decisions about the manner and timing of one's own death (Seale 2000).

As with the precise definition of birth, however, the enlargement of scientific and therapeutic knowledge and the advance of technology raise questions about the definition of death. Before the advent of sophisticated intensive care technology, patients were declared dead when breathing and cardiac activity had stopped. Since it became possible to maintain these functions artificially, a clear boundary between life and death has become less apparent. It is questionable, in fact, whether (like the beginning of life) the end of life can ever be reduced to one point in time: death is biologically a process rather than an event. But modern techniques of 'keeping alive' demand a definition. Are people in a 'persistent vegetative state' – irrevocably unconscious and without the capacity for cognitive functioning – actually persons? Whose is the decision whether they should be kept, artificially, in this state? Their own, by their previously recorded choice, or that of their relatives, or their doctors? These decisions are rendered particularly important and uncertain because a definition of death is needed for the removal of organs for transplant surgery. Healthy and functioning organs are required, and if they are to be procured from the 'dead', a legal moment of death must be recognized.

The death of patients whose brains are irretrievably traumatized can be artificially postponed, though usually only briefly, during the process of confirmation of brain death. When a brain-dead patient is designated as an organ donor, however, biological dying is postponed for a much longer period so that the organs can be 'harvested'. As Lock (2002: 120) notes, brain-dead patients may be breathing without assistance, and to think of them as dead is entirely counterintuitive. Many questions are raised:

> When do individuals or persons – as opposed to bodies – die? and how does individual death relate to the moment or process in which the vital essence 'leaves' the physical body and ceases to exist? What relationship is there among death

as a familial and social event, death of the person, and phys-
ical death? Is one form of death given priority over others?
And what moral status is assigned to each of these deaths?
(Lock 2002: 120).

It is notable that, as Lock discusses, different moments are
identified in different Western nations. The concept of 'brain
death' – that is, that death occurs at the moment when the
brain becomes irreversibly damaged – is apparently acceptable in many cultures, since high proportions of populations
say that they would not wish to be 'kept alive' in such
circumstances. Since the Brain Death Formulation of the
Medical Royal Colleges in the UK (1979) and the Uniform
Determination of Death Act (1981) in the USA, brain-dead
persons in these countries are no longer considered as living
persons. On the other hand, it is not universally acceptable,
and when the actual moment of decision arrives for relatives
at the bedside, they require to have absolute confidence in
doctors' judgement and the technology which is defining
death. Even greater problems are raised by the technique of
'non-heart-beating cadaver donors', where patients are trans-
fused with cold fluids immediately after cardiopulmonary
death, so that organs remain in good condition until they can
be removed.

The problems of both birth and death are combined with
the possibility of 'foetal rescue', the keeping of a brain-dead
mother alive in order to deliver a foetus. Definitions of
birth and death, and of 'the person', are also raised by the
use of cells from foetuses or stillborn infants for genetic
therapy, or the possibility of using anencephalic infants as
organ donors.

Changing boundaries between self and not-self

Assisted reproductive technologies, organ donation, and
replacement of body parts artificially are also examples of
technological developments associated with transformations
of the body. The healthy body becomes more widely defined

to include supplementation – the mechanical supplementation of artificial joints, ear implants, lenses for eyes, biochemical supplementation with drugs to cure imbalances, and
physiological supplementation by the transplant of organs. A
vast array of technologies becomes available to alter bodies
– what Williams (1997) calls the 'transhuman bodyshop'. The
body becomes increasingly 'bionic'. In 'cyber-medicine', with
machine parts integrated into the body, human and machine
become less and less distinct: technologies such as cardiac
pace-makers and valves, colchear implants, or insulin pumps
can imitate organic function and work with the body's own
feedback system.

These contemporary medical practices, rather than challenging mind/body divisions, 'actually exacerbate them
through a high-tech form of neo-Platonism' (Williams 1997:
1047). Organ transplants raise the mind/body dualism in a
stark form: the heart becomes 'only a pump', a spare part,
and not part of identity. Despite the many decades of discussion of the body as not a machine, of the way in which body
and mind, or body and identity, cannot be separated, transplantation suggests that the body is not the same as the self.
It is objectified: something which is possessed rather than
something that one 'is'. Body parts may fail and need to be
replaced; the body is a repairable machine. As Waldby (1998:
228) notes, medical technologies can never be understood as
simply tools like other tools, because 'it is difficult to sustain
a sense that "we" are the masters of medical technology when
"we" are also its material objects'.

As the previous discussion of 'brain death' indicated, the
brain has now taken over from the soul as the site of 'personhood', and it follows that having someone else's cornea or
kidney is not thought to threaten the authentic 'self' – even
face transplants, in the first decade of this century, have
become not only practicable but acceptable, Nevertheless, it
is commonly noted that there can be some feeling among
those who receive organ transplants that, contrary to the
machine metaphor, organs may transfer the donor's qualities
to the recipient (Sanner 2001). This may be seen as a sort of
magical thinking, beneath the surface of science (Sharp 1995),
though it is also fostered by some practices in transplantation
medicine:

> On the one hand, the language of medicine insists that human
> body parts are material entities, devoid of identity whether
> located in donors or recipients. However, in the rhetoric pro
> moting donation, organs are animated with a life force, and
> donor families are not discouraged from thinking of their
> relatives as 'living on' in the bodies of recipients. Organ dona-
> tion is very often understood as creating meaning out of
> senseless, accidental, horrifying death – a technological path
> to transcendence. All that donor families can hope for in the
> way of a return gift for this selfless act, however, is a letter of
> heartfelt thanks, often belated, written anonymously, and
> delivered through the local transplant coordination service
> with all identifying features deleted. . . . Reciprocity is reduced
> to an act of the imagination. (Lock 2002: 319)

Certainly some organs such as the heart are felt as more
central to 'self' than others such as the kidney, and are harder
to accept. There is evidence that organ recipients commonly
experience identification with the donor, or a sometimes
guilty sense that their health is at the expense of another life.

This suggests that there are still problems about the objectification of body parts. Despite the great need for organ
donors – estimated, for instance, at approximately 100,000
people waiting for some form of organ transplant in the USA
in 2007 – surveys of public opinion show that though people
support donation in principle, only a minority are prepared
to donate their own organs or consent to donation from
relatives. The giving of part of oneself can be represented as
an altruistic choice, or even in some circumstances a duty,
but it also depends on absolute trust in the medical establish-
ment. It can also come uncomfortably close to the commercial arena. Certainly commodification of body parts – their
buying and selling as commercial products – is anathema in
the West (though it has to be noted that in many places blood
is treated as a commodity). The possibility of exploitation of
the poor, in developing nations, raises recurrent scandals.
Nevertheless the logic of transferable parts from one body to
another inevitably implies some return to reductionist models
of the self. It also implies – indeed demands – new forms of
public regulation.

Interchangeability crosses species in the case of *xenotransplantation*, where transgenic animals (specially bred to carry

genes from another species) are used as donors. The shortage of supply of human organs for transplantation has led to the exploration of the use of animals as a source of tissues and organs, for instance, the transplantation of pig heart valves into humans. This has been fostered since the 1980s by the introduction of immunosuppressive drugs which make success more likely. Studies show that the willingness to receive animal organs is considerably less than for receiving human organs, though other remedies of animal origin have long been accepted: incorporation of animal organs is seen as somehow challenging one's humanity. Animals may also be used for tissue engineering, though there is the promise of replacing the need for either human donors or those from other species by the actual fabrication of organs by using biodegradable plastics as substrates for cell culture, integrated into the body.

Xenotransplantation has particular relevance for the issue of 'self and not-self'. Some problems are raised by the technique, especially the possibility of ready transfer of viruses from animals to humans. The main concern of critics is, however, ethical: that it offends the sanctity of both human and animal life by blurring species boundaries. In particular, even if the use of organs or tissues can be seen as simply mechanical 'repair', the more recent progression into the transplantation of neural cells from one species to another, with the prospect of alleviating conditions such as Huntingdon's and Parkinson's Diseases, has psychological overtones and has caused special dispute: the procedures may seem to directly affect personhood.

Stem cell technology is another development which is held to offer the promise of transformation of the way in which organs or tissue for transplantation are produced: 'from a social economy in which citizens donate whole organs to one in which embryos are a major source' (Waldby 2002). Stem cells – cells which maintain the developmental potential to become almost any kind of tissue in the body – might in future be induced to differentiate on demand, producing an unlimited supply of transplantable tissue.

They also offer revolutionary therapeutic advances. Examples commonly cited include the use of insulin-secreting cells for diabetes, nerve cells in stroke, or liver cells to repair a damaged liver. Foetal neural transplantation, or grafting of cells into the brain of an adult as a therapeutic approach to brain damage and to neurodegenerative diseases including Alzheimer's, is one of the foremost current areas of research in biology. The use of embryos, for instance embryos 'left over' from IVF, for these purposes is seen by some as ethically problematic. Positions vary in different countries, depending on attitudes to life and death issues, from the prohibition of all research to the complete acceptance of the creation of embryos for these purposes. Similarly, cloning techniques, and the birth of new siblings from selected embryos specifically so that cells might be retrieved from the umbilical cord to 'treat' the disease of existing children, are controversial. But what, Waldby asks:

> . . . does it mean when the human body can be disaggregated into fragments that are derived from a particular person, but are no longer constitutive of human identity? . . . What is the status of such fragments, and how is the status of the individual (strictly speaking, the in-dividual, he who cannot be subdivided) altered to accommodate these possibilities for fragmentation? (Waldby 2002: 308)

Changing boundaries between therapy and enhancement

In addition to these therapeutic developments, in an age of commercial 'healthism', body maintenance and plastic surgery, the *healthy* body also becomes plastic and can be reshaped and transformed. As Glasner (1995: 175) comments:

> If the period from the mid-1800s to the mid-1900s was one in which the individual's body became a vehicle for the display of consumer products, lately we are faced with the next logical step in consumerism. No longer can we merely dress up the body we happen to have, or improve it by losing weight or having a beauty makeover or straightening out the curve in our nose. We must actually purchase a 'new body'.

The distinction between therapeutic procedures aimed at restoring individuals to normality, and enhancement procedures aimed at improving them beyond the normal, is becoming difficult to sustain:

> The possibilities are immense – from augmenting memory at one extreme through to attempts at endless extension of the human lifespan at the other. The criteria for determining the boundaries of normality and human nature are unclear, and, therefore, so are the dimensions of therapy. How can we know when we have moved from therapy to enhancement? (Jones and Whitaker 2009: 282)

A movement known as trans- or post-humanism in fact promotes the use of technological means to create 'post humans' or 'trans humans' by pushing the natural boundaries far beyond current human expectations (Bostrum 2005).

At a more every-day level, there is an area of confusion between high-tech 'enhancement' such as the use of steroids in athletics or the use of chemical mood-enhancers, and low-tech 'interventions' such as nutritional supplements. The former are regarded as 'unnatural', and a common suggestion is that enhancement interventions may produce or worsen inequalites. The latter are considered morally unproblematic, though they could equally be relevant to inequality.

Much of the debate about enhancement concerns the modification of the brain through psychopharmaceuticals, or 'cosmetic neurology'. Pharmaceuticals can 'treat' everything from sleepiness to insomnia, and forgetfulness to shyness and mild depression. The line between therapy and enhancement is usually drawn by the distinction between normality and abnormality, health and disease. But this distinction, as discussed in chapter 1, is awkward and unclear.

The 'lifestyle' use of pharmaceuticals to satisfy non-health-related goals is another contribution to the blurring of the distinction between ill and not-ill. Drugs developed to treat extreme states or formally acknowledged diseases (for instance, Alzheimers, Hyperactivity and Attention Deficit Disorders, or the treatment of excessive daytime sleepiness such as experienced in narcolepsy) are widely employed by healthy individuals for non-medical reasons. Products designed to aid weight loss in clinically obese patients are widely used to sustain low weight, and drugs designed for erectile disfunction are used 'recreationally' to aid sexual performance. On the other hand, drugs which are designed as lifestyle aids encourage the definition of new 'diseases'. Fox and Ward (2009) suggest that we are seeing the pharmaceuticalization of daily life. With direct marketing to the consumer, where this is legally possible, and supply via the internet, drugs can be acquired privately and consumed domestically.

These new technologies generally not only blur the distinction between body and not-body, ill and not-ill, but call into question human relationships. Fox and Ward (2009: 50) show how

> ... the social relations surrounding contemporary pharmaceutical production and consumption link the world of business to the private worlds of citizens, forging new diseases and treatments from the very fabric of daily life.

Health becomes personalized, as well as individualized.

Information technologies and medical practice

The combination of 'hard' technologies and new therapies with 'softer' technologies such as information systems also changes the definition of the patient and the medical task. The use of telemedicine, or information technology used to support the delivery of health services, has been actively supported by health policy in Western medical systems for at least a decade. There are new kinds of links between clinicians and patients which mean that they need have no physical contact. This is attractive to policy, because it may offer solutions to some of the problems of access to care. It obviously has special application in places where population densities or special environments create problems for the supply of specialist services, such as Arctic areas and parts of Australia, the United States and Canada. Medical telemetry (images and readings sent electronically), already part of space medicine, means that consultation (perhaps between several people) can take place at a distance. There can be 'automated' consultation, which means that personal contact need not be involved at all, or at least that patients can be screened before the involvement of a clinician. 'Virtual surgery' can be performed at a distance, and whole new disciplines such as teleradiology or teledentistry evolve.

Indeed, a whole new field of knowledge around the new information technologies in medicine has emerged, with new journals devoted to its knowledge base. At the level of the patient, new forms of communication provide a wider access to information: privileged access to knowledge is no longer the exclusive mark of the doctor, and the Internet loosens the boundaries between the lay person and the professional.

All this requires, however, a standardization of medicine. It implies agreement on evidence-based clinical facts and cannot be totally flexible. May et al. (2001) offer the example of the introduction of a relatively low-tech experimental videophone system, designed to facilitate the referral of patients with anxiety and depression in primary care to a community health team. They point out that there can be conflict between the 'hard' technology – the computer or videophone – and the 'soft' – the body of knowledge and the skills and interactional practices of doctors. In this instance there were some reservations about the system on the part of doctors.

Moreover, the new imaging technologies tend to require very specialized knowledge, not universally shared. Prior et al. show how the new technologies and the new genetics come together when risks are 'assembled' in a cancer genetics clinic. Both computer programmes of family histories and techniques of producing images of DNA sequences require expert knowledge for their interpretation, and 'even though clinicians and laboratory professionals understand what goes on in the lab they understand it in different ways' (Prior et al. 2002: 255). At each stage there is potential for seeing and assessing in different ways and from different standpoints. Making things 'visible' has to be of paramount importance.

The new hard technologies favour specialities that use primarily on-screen data or images, or those where all the data can be seen as objective and measurable, rather than those that focus on the direct examination of patients in the context of their lives. Wyatt (1996) suggests that these developments are fundamentally 'technologically pulled' rather than 'clinically pushed' and inevitably produce pressures towards the standardization of disease symptoms and categories. All essentially 'laboratory' medicine, as May et al. (2001) notes, also breaks the immediate connection between consultation and diagnosis, which can be seen as attacking the whole culture of medical space and medical presence.

'Evidence-based medicine' (EBM) is a contemporary movement extremely popular in Western medicine, which also produces pressures towards the standardization of symptoms and disease and some potential distancing between the doctor and the patient. Organizational reliance on 'systematic reviews' of scientific evidence of the efficacy and efficiency of drugs and procedures can be seen as a form of 'soft' technology designed to reduce variation, achieve equity in access to treatment, provide checks and balances, and use resources in the most effective and efficient way. From the point of view of clinicians, it can provide objective standards and assist in decision-making by diffusing responsibility. If introduced too formally into health-care systems, however, the natural consequence is a protocol-driven medicine which can tend to abstract the definition of health and disease from the individual patient. Diagnoses are created by fiat, rather than judgement of individual cases. In addition, EBM can offer scientific legitimation for financial and political regulation of the distribution of health care. Thus it becomes another example of the effects of technology in changing definitions of the patient and diseases.

Changing attitudes to health and medicine

At the same time, the postmodern world is marked by what is spoken of as the 'end of tradition'. This includes a loss of faith in those traditionally seen as experts, including the medical profession. People are encouraged to make their own decisions – what the British sociologist Giddens calls the 'reflexivity of the self' – based on ever more numerous sources of information. Issues of health are increasingly attractive to the mass media, and bodies of information range from self-help manuals of all kinds to the changing, flexible, not always clearly legitimized World Wide Web. As Hardey (1999) has commented, the users of information, rather than the professional experts, begin to decide what is to be delivered to them. Traditionally, health education is directed and distributed by doctors and educators, but the Internet offers a view of health which is 'deprofessionized and demystified', making the provisional nature of medical knowledge more obvious.

There is a blurring of lay and medical knowledge. Debates about medical knowledge and medical ethics are made more public. At the same time that medicine becomes more 'scientific' and technological, a pluralistic view of health is encouraged, since information is supplied about different medical systems, and lay 'stories' begin to be included. There is greater openness towards complementary and alternative therapies, and increasing interest in them among a consumerist public, shopping for care and cure.

All this reflects profound changes in medicine and in attitudes to health. The 'old' biomedical health care was characterized as curative, based in structures and institutions, and with the interaction between doctors and patients at its core. 'New' or postmodern medicine is preventive, not institutionalized, and multidisciplinary. Leisure is an industry, health promotion is individualized, and health itself is an international commodity. As Bunton and Burrows commented (1995: 207), 'health is idealized as self-governed lifestyle choice'. We live, as Wilkinson describes, in a 'cash and keys' society, constantly exposed to pressures from the market and constantly monitoring our own position in that market:

> Whenever we leave the confines of our own homes we face the world with the two perfect symbols of the nature of social relations on the street. Cash equips us to take part in transactions mediated by the market, while keys protect our private gains from each other's envy and greed. What adds to the social potency of these arrangements is that instead of being marginal to our lives, they are the organizing principles of the most highly interdependent system of production and consumption that has ever existed. Although we are all wholly dependent on one another for our livelihoods, this interdependence is turned from being a social process into a process by

which we fend for ourselves in an attempt to wrest a living from an asocial environment. Instead of being people with whom we have social bonds and share common interests, others become rivals, competitors for jobs, for houses, space, seats on the bus, parking places. And yet, as social beings, we cannot treat others in the arena of public life simply as part of the natural environment: instead processes of social comparison – favourable or unfavourable – mean everything is constantly monitored. (Wilkinson 1996: 226)

The new flexibility and reflexive identity do not redress the old inequalities of health that were discussed in chapter 5. New stresses arise, transformed by socio-biologic processes into disease, and

although we may well be witnessing the emergence of late modern forms of self-identity it is not a uniform transformation across the population. Some actors have a much greater autonomy to construct their identities than others. Whilst some may be able to pay for cosmetic surgery others have to wait for unacceptably long periods just for routine relief from pain and other obstacles to their daily lives. Whilst some can afford to choose extra virgin olive oil and fresh vegetables, others have to sleep in cardboard boxes on the streets and eat what food they can get. (Bunton and Burrows 1995: 211)

New technologies and the risk society

In the world of the new technologies, discourses of risk are pervasive. Since the appreciation of risk is the means by which individuals are encouraged to regulate their lives and bodies, this is associated with ideas of choice and responsibility. Framing issues in terms of risk status suggests a personal, deliberate resolution to improve one's own health. At the societal level, the imperatives which this new society requires are flexibility and a necessary amount of risk-taking.

In the 'modern', as opposed to the postmodern, world, risk was always one of the basic concepts of social epidemiology, in the form of risk factors for disease, relative risks of mortality, or predictors of particular types of ill health. Towards the end of the twentieth century, with a rising interest in the functional purposes of risk in an increasingly uncertain world, an industry developed concerned with risk and risk assessment. The 'rational' approach saw risk as a technical matter, to be tackled with more science and better information. From this point of view a basic premise is that all risks are measurable and possible to control. People's own perceptions of risk were not, it was recognized, necessarily in the same rational frame, and the psychology of risk or the relationship between lay and expert perceptions of risk became a prolific field of research. Anthropology pointed out that risks are culturally constructed, and variations in risk recognition and response are the products of different cultures, institutions and lifestyles (Douglas 1992).

Douglas had earlier formalized a schema (Douglas 1970) to analyse how people identified different risks in the context of their own form of social organization. This came to be known as grid/group analysis: 'grid' means 'the social distinctions and delegations of authority that they use to limit how people behave to one another', and 'group' is 'the outside boundary that people have erected between themselves and the outside world' (Douglas and Wildavsky 1982: 138). By combining grid and group, four distinct 'cultural biases' are identified in the context of risk, which were called hierarchist, egalitarian, fatalist and individualist. The implications of this were that people choose (not necessarily consciously) attitudes to risk and different types of behaviour which are most suitable for their own social organization and way of life.

In its specific application to health, this attention to the concept of risk is an essential part of the 'surveillance society'. Risk is the language of health education. Individualized 'risk factors' – smoking, overweight, a sedentary lifestyle – became almost synonymous with disease. This emphasis on potentially deviant practices and lifestyles, defining them as risky or not, has been described by Clarke (2003) as *biomedicalization*, and contrasted with the earlier process of medicalization. Now, 'risk-medicine' fights against uncertainty, and prognosis of probable futures defines a person's present health status. There can be resistance to this, as there has been to medicalization.

The perception and management of voluntary risks, and the relative importance of these lifestyle factors and other environmentally and socially imposed health risks, thus become the central questions of health promotion and public health. As Prior (2000) notes, even the certainty of death is transformed into a private risk: death is no longer capricious and random, but simply a 'risk' which is in our own hands, with some sense of ultimate avoidability:

> Death, it seems, stalks only those that are careless of their own personal health. This, despite the fact that the mortality rates of those who are careless of their health and those who are fastidious remain stubbornly similar (viz 100 per cent). It is perhaps a frame of mind summarised by the use among epidemiologists of the phrase 'avoidable death' – you too can avoid death if you have behaved yourself. (Prior 2000: 193)

Expert and lay frames with regard to risk are, of course, bound to differ, and the concept of risk is inevitably full of paradox. The probabilities produced by risk analysis relate to groups, and can say nothing about the individual case. Given a relatively rare health event associated with common behaviours or characteristics, while most of those who experience it may have been 'at risk', most of those at risk will escape the event. In the case of risk status for coronary disease, for instance, Davison et al. (1991: 15) demonstrated the prevalence of the idea of 'coronary candidacy', based on the wide range of conditions and behaviours that people had been taught, or had perceived through their own experience, as being causally linked to the onset of heart disease but recognized as not *necessary* causes:

> The candidacy system, then, has two interwoven strands. On the one hand is a set of criteria which can be used in the post-hoc explanation of illness and death, the prediction of illness and death, and the assessment of risk. On the other hand, there exists the all-important knowledge that the system is fallible. It cannot account for all coronary disease and death, neither can it account for the apparently unwarranted longevity of some of those that the system itself labels as candidates. Thus the observation that 'it never seems to happen to the

people you expect it to happen to' becomes integrated as a central part of the system itself.

In part as a consequence of the limitations for epidemiology of the conventional individualized risk approach – it has been suggested, for instance, that when all known risk factors for coronary heart disease are considered together, they account for only about 40 per cent of the incidence of the disease – wider issues in postmodern society come to the fore. The concept of the 'risk society' (Beck 1992) has been particularly influential. Beck suggests that we live in a society which is increasingly interdependent, increasingly vulnerable to international catastrophe and to the risk management of organizations over which we have no control. Health risks – especially ecological, genetic, nuclear, but also the economic risks associated with global economies – are in the hands of 'experts' whose manner of assessment we may not even understand, and whom we may not trust. The erosion of trust is fostered by the growing recognition that these risks are often ultimately unknowable.

There is nothing new, of course, about the fact that life presents continual risks to the health of the individual, or that medicine has always been based on risk assessments. The safety and efficacy of treatments have always had to be balanced. The new technologies develop new iatrogenic risks, however: their risk profiles tend to be narrower. There is also change in the way in which the imposition of technological risks is recognized, publicized, feared and resisted by the population. Governments assume a duty to take preventive action, not usually by removing the risks but by suggesting ways of accommodating them. So potassium iodide is stored to be distributed to families within two kilometres of nuclear power stations against the possibility, however remote, of accident; in periods of perceived high risk of terrorist attack in public places the public are warned to be individually vigilant; travellers by air are recommended to use aspirin and compression stockings to guard against deep vein thrombosis. Simply to live in one's house, or journey to work, or travel abroad, is to expose oneself to harm-in-waiting. Not to take precautions against risks which may be quite remote is seen

as dereliction of duty on the part of governments and care-
lessness on the part of individuals.

At the same time the possibility of approaching health risks
in their own lives rationally, and attempting to control them,
is not evenly distributed in the population, so new forms of
inequality, 'the inequality of dealing with insecurity and
reflexivity', are created:

> The social positions and conflicts of a 'wealth-distributing
> society' become joined by those of a 'risk-distributing society';
> social risk positions spring up, which are not exactly class
> positions, but which are associated with them because the
> ability to deal with risk is unequally distributed in occupa-
> tional and educational groups. (Beck 1992: 20)

Evolutionary medicine

The trends which have been considered – the postmodern
changes in self and society, the rise of the risk society, and in
particular the new genetics – lead, finally, to the most specu-
lative developments in the contemporary definition of health,
concerned with the 'new Darwinism' and what is called evolutionary medicine. These relate to quite fundamental changes
in ideas about the public health and, indeed, the future of
humankind.

An earlier, and not universally acceptable, version of this
was the movement known as socio-biology. This applies to
human behaviour the Darwinian thesis that organisms must
maximize their reproductive success. Genes that enable individuals to survive, within a particular environment, and have
more offspring will increase over time as the result of natural
selection. A basic tenet is that individuals, and hence their
genes, are self-benefiting (described by the biologist Dawkins
as the 'selfish gene'), and thus traits favourable for selection
in the past will condition current behaviour. Individuals are
genetically predisposed to certain behaviours because these
maximized the fitness of their ancestors over previous generations. A corollary is that, when the environment changes,
certain genes may become less well adapted.

In its crudest form, sociobiology was criticized as deterministic, and the Darwinian 'survival of the fittest' metaphor rejected as appearing to justify inequality or even racial discrimination. There were problems in talking of 'universal' human traits, in view of the diversity of human societies and behaviour. In particular, in classical Darwinian terms, it is heresy to ascribe intentionality or to assume that the existence of a characteristic is evidence that it must have evolved 'for a purpose': evolution is based on the occurrence of random variations between individuals, which either enhance or reduce chances of surviving (in a changing environment) to reproduce and pass genetic characteristics on to offspring.

More sophisticated forms of social Darwinism are exemplified by, for instance, Dickens (2000: 116), who suggests how 'evolutionary thought and social theory can be combined' by considering the way in which 'capital is modifying human biological structure in its own image'. Human biology evolves not by simple accident, but by manipulation – that is, by the exercise of social power. There is not only the possibility of deliberate genetic or other biological manipulation, but also a more subtle process – a 'gradual embedding' of a division between abstract and concrete thinking in the biological structure of the population. The power structure of modern society means that conceptual work is highly prized and rewarded, and practical work downgraded. Thus the social and the biological meet in selection according to certain types of aptitude and ability.

The movement known as evolutionary ecology distinguishes itself from social Darwinism, focusing on the interactions between the individual and the organism in specific environments. From this perspective, health is in part contingent on the difference between modern environments and those in which humankind evolved. It is observed that diseases have their own evolutionary history: the characteristics of diseases, as well as of individuals, are the products or by-products of adaptation by natural selection in a particular environment. Chisholm (1998) gives examples of the way in which various symptoms of 'pathology' are actually defence mechanisms, adaptive responses to a new environment. Fever in response to infection, women's reproductive cancers in modern industrial societies, pregnancy sickness, infant colic

– all are pathologies which can be reinterpreted as adaptation to a changing environment:

> when people lack the resources to limit environmental risk and uncertainty they may be induced to grow and come to behave (most of the time probably quite unconsciously) in ways associated with earlier and/or frequent reproduction – even at the cost of decreased health, wellbeing and shortened lives. From an evolutionary perspective, this makes sense. Natural selection favours reproductive capacity, not health. (Chisholm 1998: 84)

As Chisholm points out, evolutionary theory can alter fundamentally the way we think about health and disease. There is tension between ends and means: having descendants, not health, is the 'goal' of life, and health is not always the best measure of adaptation. Questions are raised about the 'normal'. 'Evolutionary medicine' is about

> . . . exploring the implications for therapy of understanding the processes of adaptation that produce the evolutionary histories that culminate in a particular person, presenting with a particular complaint, at a particular place and time. (Chisholm 1998: 73–4)

Fundamental questions are now raised about the basic concepts of agent, environment and host. The aim of public health becomes the reduction of environmental risk and uncertainty in order to achieve control over adaptation to change.

Conclusion

Western medicine, in the period which this volume has particularly considered, was founded in a very particular view of the world, that of the scientific biomedical model. At the beginning of the twenty-first century it seems, in Chisholm's words, 'poised to take the radical philosophical step of exploring how modern evolutionary theory might augment these venerable ways of knowing' (1998: 72). Many of the changes which have been discussed – new technologies and developments in the organization of medicine, new ways of seeing the body, postmodern fragmentation and flux, and confusion of the self and not-self, body and not-body – are altering the way in which health is perceived. The old certainties of single causes, generic diseases, the definition of ill health as deviation from the normal – even the doctrine of scientific neutrality – are all seen as problematic, and the pace of change leaves many contradictions and dilemmas.

There are, as always, tensions between the individual and the public health. The new genetics is promulgated as offering the most promising cure for disease: that is, gene therapy is marketed as having personal benefits for the individual and for potential offspring. It has been argued that this benefit is not always clear, since most diseases of the modern world are not genetic in a way that invites simple therapies. Nevertheless it is legitimated in terms of population benefits: the old concept of the magic bullet resurrected. The more simplistic idea that there is a quick fix associated with defective genes reinforces the definition of health and illness as related to individual characteristics rather than the social environment. In a sense this is the concept of health turning back to itself. Holistic medicine embraced a model of the healthy individual as a social whole, but here the body is being atomized down to its smallest components – which, in the end, represent its personal genetic uniqueness.

Further reading

Beck, U. 1992: *Risk Society: Towards a New Modernity*. London: Sage.

Faulkner, A. 2009: *Medical Technology, Healthcare and Society: A Sociology of Devices, Innovation and Governance*. Basingstoke: Palgrave Macmillan.

Kerr, A. and Shakespeare, T. 2002: *Genetic Politics: From Eugenics to Genome*. Cheltenham: New Clarendon Press.

Lehoux, P. 2006: *The Problem of Health Technology*. Abingdon: Routledge.

Lock, M. 2002: *Twice Dead: Organ Transplants and the Reinvention of Death*. Berkeley and Los Angeles: University of California Press.

Williams, S. J., Birke, L. and Bendelow, G. 2003: *Debating Biology. Sociological Reflections on Health, Medicine and Society*. London: Routledge.

Williams, S. J., Gabe J. and Calnan, M. (eds) 2000: *Health, Medicine and Society: Key Theories, Future Agenda*s. London: Routledge.

7
Conclusion

This discussion of the meaning of 'health' began with some simple definitions expressed in lay accounts, and concludes with speculations about the difficulties created for lay people by the technological and other changes in the modern world. Throughout history, health has always been a slightly slippery concept, with, as chapter 1 discussed, a variety of meanings. No single definition has been offered here, for the theme of the book has been not only that a single all purpose definition of health is impossible, but that attempts to impose one have never been very functional.

One of the most pervasive ideas has always been some concept of normality, though what is normal is obviously historically specific, culturally defined, and dependent on the state of knowledge at the time. Health has commonly been defined in functional terms, as the efficiency of bodily systems and fitness for the tasks that people want to perform, as balance or homeostasis, as psychosocial feelings of well-being or happiness, or for more than a century in Western societies as not diseased, injured, or otherwise malfunctioning according to a 'medical model' associated with the science and profession of medicine. Consideration of the way that the concept has changed throughout history and has developed in different cultures demonstrates its shifting nature, and the now extensive body of research on lay formulations and beliefs shows how clearly these are patterned not only by history but also by characteristics such as age and gender and the circumstances of people's lives. An important point which has been made is that neither in lay perceptions, nor as manifested in their actual experience, are health and illness simply logical opposites.

These ideas are important to those who try to cure disease, and to those who influence the policy of health services. People's actions, including their help-seeking behaviour, how they act when they are ill, and their health-harming or health-protecting lifestyles, are all affected by the way in which they perceive that disease is caused and health is manifested. Chapter 4 began to introduce questions of structure and agency with regard to health, or the extent to which health is determined by forces outside the individual's control or, alternatively, is in their own hands.

Questions were also raised about the extent to which health is nowadays defined by the governments who exercise surveillance over it and by the commercial interests who turn it into a commodity. Chapter 5 turned more explicitly to health as a social and political issue, and the way in which individual experience may be the product of a society's resources and the way they are organized. Explanations have to be sought for the differences between countries in general levels of health, and between groups within countries. The perception and definition of health inequalities, and particularly the study of their causes, leads to new theories of what health is and how it is determined. Here, ideas about the 'socio-biologic translation' by which stresses are thought to become manifest in disease, the concept of social capital, and newer critiques of this neo-liberal position were introduced.

Finally, chapter 6 considered the place of health in the 'risk society' and its definition in postmodern societies undergoing flux and change. The blurring of the clear distinctions between ill and not-ill, self and not-self, life and not-life all require new ethical considerations. In previous eras, it is difficult to think of scientific discoveries and technological breakthroughs in the field of health where the ethical questions is not 'how can we afford, or how should we distribute, the fruits of this life-saving or enhancing advance?', but 'is it ethical to make use of this new knowledge?' Any definition of disease as deviation from the normal, with the purpose of medical therapy as the restoration of normality, is unsettled: many new technologies offer the possibility of enhancing the normal. At the same time as consumerist society puts ever greater emphasis on medicine and what it can achieve, the idea of health as a universally prior value is questioned. Defined simply as the absence of disease or illness it is – as lay accounts have always declared – not the only or uncomplicated goal of life.

One theme throughout has been that health is (in people's perceptions, as well as logically) a positive state, different from the simple absence of illness or disease. But this positive concept becomes ever more complex and difficult to define. More and more, it appears to be an interaction between people and their environment. This resonates with the experience of health as both inside and outside the self, but how it affects the apparently fundamental perception of the moral nature of health is not yet clear: all that is obvious is that there are new moral issues.

The theme of choice and responsibility has been pervasive throughout this volume, in relation to health policy and also to the way in which health is experienced. The emphasis of self-determination and the enhancement of freedom of choice in the discussion of the new genetics again reflects an increasing emphasis on active citizenship in Western societies. Policy turns particularly to creating conditions that allow and enable self-government. However, at the same time genetics individualizes, placing ill health firmly within rather than without, but also removing active responsibility. How individuals struggle with this dilemma is not very well understood. There is in fact some argument that the mere availability of new technologies creates pressures for their use, and some concern that they may allow governments, commercial interests and the scientific community to market their own objectives under the banner of therapy and consumer choice.

It is hardly original to note that the pace of change is accelerating, but it is perhaps important to point to the variety of forces driving change, and that the resultant ambiguities between life and the inanimate, mind and body, the individual and public health, require continual monitoring. Meanwhile, the ill person is where he or she always was – trying to find a moral identity, trying to live in an uncertain and unreliable body, and trying to make the most of their allotted time in a changing world.

References

Antonovsky, A. 1979: *Health, Stress and Coping*. San Francisco: Jossey-Bass.

Arksey, H. 1994: Expert and lay participation in the construction of medical knowledge. *Sociology of Health and Illness*, 16, 448–68.

Armstrong, D. 1993: From clinical gaze to regime of total health. In A. Beattie, M. Gott, L. Jones and M. Sidell (eds) *Health and Wellbeing*. London: Macmillan and Open University, 55–67.

—— 1995: The rise of surveillance medicine. *Sociology of Health and Illness*, 17, 397–404.

Barr, M., and Rose, D. 2009: The great ambivalence: factors likely to affect service user and public acceptability of the pharmacogenetics of antidepressant medication. In S. J. Williams, J. Gabe and P. Davis (eds) *Pharmaceuticals and Society: Critical Discourses and Debates*. Chichester: Wiley-Blackwell.

Baudrillard, J. 1983: *Simulations*. New York: Semiotext.

Bauman, B. 1961: Diversities in conceptions of health and physical fitness. *Journal of Health and Human Behaviour*, 2, 39–47.

Beck, U. 1992: *Risk Society: Towards a New Modernity*. London: Sage.

Becker, H. S. 1963: *Outsiders: Studies in the Sociology of Deviance*. New York: Free Press.

Berg, M., and Bowker, G. 1997: The multiple bodies of the medical record: towards a sociology of an artifact. *The Sociological Quarterly*, 38, 311–35.

Berg, M., and Mol, A. M. (eds) 1998: *Differences in Medicine. Unravelling Techniques, Practices and Bodies*. Durham, NC: Duke University Press.

Bergholt, K. 2006: *Wellbeing: A Cultural History of Healthy Living.* Cambridge: Polity.

Blair, A. 1993: Social class and the contextualization of illness experience. In A. Radley (ed.) *Worlds of Illness: Biographical and Cultural Perspectives on Health and Disease.* London: Routledge, 27–48.

Blane, D., Brunner, E., and Wilkinson, R. 1996: *Health and Social Organisation.* London: Routledge.

Blaxter, M. 1978: Diagnosis as category and process: the case of alcoholism. *Social Science and Medicine,* 12, 9–17.

—— 1983: The causes of disease: women talking. *Social Science and Medicine,* 1, 59–69.

—— 1990: *Health and Lifestyles.* London: Routledge.

—— 1993: Why do the victims blame themselves? In A. Radley (ed.) *Worlds of Illness: Biographical and Cultural Perspectives on Health and Disease.* London: Routledge, 124–42.

—— 2000: Class, time and biography. In S. J. Williams, J. Gabe and M. Calnan (eds) *Health, Medicine and Society: Key Theories, Future Agendas.* London: Routledge, 27–50.

—— 2003: Biology, social class and inequalities in health: their synthesis in 'health capital'. In S. J. Williams, L. Birke and G. Bendelow, *Debating Biology.* London: Routledge, 69–83.

—— 2004: Life narratives, health and identity. In Kelleher, D. and Leavey, G., *Identity and Health.* London: Routledge.

Blaxter, M., and Paterson, E. 1982: *Mothers and Daughters: A Three-Generational Study of Health Attitudes and Behaviour.* London: Heinemann.

Blaxter, M., and Poland, F. 2002: Moving beyond the survey in exploring social capital. In C. Swann and A. Morgan (eds) *Social Capita for Health, Insights from Qualitative Research.* London: Health Development Agency.

Blumer, H. 1969: *Symbolic Interactionism.* Englewood Cliffs, NJ: Prentice-Hall.

Bobak, M., Pikhart, H., Rose, R., Hertzman, C., and Marmot, M. 2000: Socioeconomic factors, material inequalities, and perceived control in self-rated health: cross-sectional data from seven post-communist countries. *Social Science and Medicine,* 51, 1343– 50.

Bostrum, N. 2005: In defense of posthuman dignity, *Bioethics,* 19, 202–14.

Bourdieu, P. 1984: *Distinction: A Social Critique of the Judgement of Taste.* London: Routledge.

Bunton, R., and Burrows, R. 1995: Consumption and health in the 'epidemiological' clinic of late modern medicine. In R. Bunton,

S. Nettleton and R. Burrows (eds) *The Sociology of Health Promotion*. London: Routledge, 206–22.

Bury, M. 1982: Chronic illness as biographical disruption, *Sociology of Health and Illness*, 4, 167–82.

—— 2001: Illness narratives: fact or fiction? *Sociology of Health and Illness*, 23, 263–85.

—— 2005: *Health and Illness*. Cambridge: Polity.

Bury, M., and Wadsworth, M. 2003: The biological clock: ageing, health and the body across the lifecourse. In S. J. Williams, L. Birke and G. A. Bendelow, *Debating Biology*. London: Routledge 109–20.

Calnan, M. 1987: *Health and Illness: The Lay Perspective*. London: Tavistock.

Chisholm, J. 1998: Evolutionary medicine. In A. Petersen and C. Waddell (eds) *Health Matters*. Buckingham: Open University Press, 72–87.

Chrysanthou, M. 2002: Transparency and selfhood: utopia and the informed body. *Social Science and Medicine*, 54, 469–79.

Clarke, A. E. 2003: Biomedicalisation: technoscientific transformation of health, illness and disease. *American Sociological Review*, 68, 161–94.

Coburn, D. 2000: Income inequality, social cohesion and the health status of populations: the role of neo-liberalism. *Social Science and Medicine*, 51, 135–46.

Cockerham, W. C. 2007: *Social Causes of Health and Disease*. Cambridge: Polity.

Coleman, J. S. 1988: Social capital in the creation of human capital. *American Journal of Sociology*, S95–120.

Conrad, P. 1999: A mirage of genes. *Sociology of Health and Illness*, 21, 228–41.

—— 2007: *The Medicalization of Society*. Baltimore: Johns Hopkins University Press.

Cornwell, J. 1984: *Hard-Earned Lives: Accounts of Health and Illness from East London*. London: Tavistock.

Cox, B., Huppert, F. A., and Wichelow, M. 1993: *The Health and Lifestyle Survey: Seven Years On*. Aldershot: Dartmouth.

Cox, S., and McKellin, W. 1999: 'There's this thing in our family': predictive testing and the construction of risk for Huntington's Disease. *Sociology of Health and Illness*, 21, 622–46.

Crawford, R. 1977: You are dangerous to your health: the ideology and politics of victim blaming. *International Journal of Health Services*, 7, 663–78.

—— 1984: A cultural account of 'health': control, release and the social body. In J. B. McKinlay (ed.) *Issues in the Political*

Economy of Health Care. London: Tavistock; abridged in A. Beattie, M. Gott, L. Jones and M. Sidell (1993) (eds) *Health and Wellbeing*. *London*: Macmillan Press and Open University, 133–43.

—— 2000: The ritual of health promotion. In S. J. Williams, J. Gabe and M. Calnan (eds) *Health, Medicine and Society: Key Theories, Future Agendas*. London: Routledge, 219–35.

Cregan, K. 2006: *The Sociology of the Body*. London: Sage.

Crossley, M. L. 2000: *Introducing Narrative Psychology: Self, Trauma and the Construction of Meaning*. Buckingham: Open University Press.

Daly, J. 1989: Innocent murmurs: echocardiography and the diagnosis of cardiac normality. *Sociology of Health and Illness*, 11, 99–116.

Davey Smith, G., Gunnel, D. C., and Ben-Shlomo, Y. 2001: Life-course approaches to socio-economic differentials in cause-specific adult mortality. In D. Leon and G. Walt (eds) *Poverty, Inequality and Health*. Oxford: Oxford University Press, 88–124.

Davison, C., Davey Smith, G., and Frankel, S. 1991: Lay epidemiology and the prevention paradox: the implications of coronary candidacy for health education. *Sociology of Health and Illness*, 13, 1–19.

Department of Health and Social Services 1980: *Inequalities in Health (Black Report)*. London: DHSS.

D'Houtard, A., and Field, M. 1986: New research on the image of health. In C. Currer and M. Stacey (eds) *Concepts of Health, Illness and Disease*. Leamington Spa: Berg.

Dickens, P. 2000: *Social Darwinism*. Milton Keynes: Open University Press.

Douglas, M. 1970: *Natural Symbols: Essays in Anthropology*. London: Routledge and Kegan Paul.

—— 1992: *Risk and Blame*. London: Routledge.

Douglas, M., and Wildavsky, A. 1982: *Risk and Culture: An Essay on the Selection of Technical and Environmental Dangers*. Berkeley: University of California Press.

Dubos, R. J. 1959: *Mirage of Health*. New York: Harper.

1965: *Man Adapting*. New Haven, CT: Yale University Press.

Ehrenreich, A., and English, D. 1978: The 'sick' women of the upper classes. In J. Ehrenreich (ed.) *The Cultural Crisis of Modern Medicine*. New York: Monthly Review Press.

Elliott, A. 2001: *Concepts of the Self*. Cambridge: Polity.

Engel, R. L. 1963: Medical diagnosis: present, past and future. *Archives of Internal Medicine*, 112, 520–9.

Erde, E. 1979: Philosophical considerations regarding defining 'health', 'disease', etc. and their bearing on medical practice. *Ethics in Science and Medicine*, 6, 31–48.

Fabrega, H. 1976a: The biological significance of taxonomies of disease. *Journal of Theoretical Biology*, 63, 191–216.

—— 1976b: Toward a theory of human disease. *Journal of Nervous and Mental Diseases*, 162, 299–312.

—— 1977: The scope of ethnomethodological science. *Culture Medicine and Psychiatry*, 1, 201–28.

Faulkner, A. 2009: *Medical Technology, Healthcare and Society: A Sociology of Devices, Innovation and Governance*. Basingstoke: Palgrave Macmillan.

Fleck, L. [1935] 1979: *Genesis and Development of a Scientific Fact*. Chicago: University of Chicago Press.

Foley, M. W., and Edwards, B. 1999: Is it time to disinvest in social capital? *Journal of Public Policy*, 19, 141–73.

Foucault, M. 1973: *The Birth of the Clinic*. London: Tavistock.

—— 1977: *Discipline and Punish: The Birth of the Prison*. London: Allen Lane.

Fox, N., and Ward, K. J. 2009: Pharma in the bedroom . . . and the kitchen . . . The pharmaceuticalisation of daily life. In S. J. Williams, J. Gabe and P. Davis (eds), *Pharmaceuticals and Society. Critical Discourses and Debates*, Chichester: Wiley-Blackwell, 41–53.

Frank, A. W. 1991: *At the Will of the Body: Reflection on Illness*. Boston: Houghton-Mifflin.

—— 1992: Twin nightmares of the medical simulacrum. In W. Stearns and W. Chaloupke (eds) *Jean Baudrillard: The Disappearance of Art and Politics*. London: Macmillan, 82–97.

—— 1995: *The Wounded Storyteller: Body, Illness and Ethics*. Chicago and London: University of Chicago Press.

Frankenberg, R. 1992: Your time or mine: temporal contradictions of biomedical practice. In R. Frankenberg (ed.) *Time, Health and Medicine*. London: Sage, 1–30.

Fraser, M., and Greco, M. (eds) 2005: *The Body: A Reader*. Abingdon: Routledge.

Freidson, E. 1960: Client control and medical practice. American Journal of *Sociology*, 65, 374–82.

—— 1965: Disability as social deviance. In M. B. Sussman (ed.) *Sociology of Disability and Rehabilitation*. Washington, DC: American Sociological Association.

Giddens, A. 1991: *Modernity and Self-Identity: Self and Society in the Late Modern Age*. Cambridge: Polity.

Glasner, B. 1995: In the name of health. In R. Bunton, S. Nettleton and R. Burrows (eds) *The Sociology of Health Promotion.* London: Routledge, 159–75.

Goffman, E. 1967: *Stigma: Notes on the Management of Spoiled Identity.* Englewood Cliffs, NJ: Prentice-Hall.

Good, B. J. 1994: *Medicine, Rationality and Experience: An Anthropological Perspective.* Cambridge: Cambridge University Press.

Green, G. 2009: *The End of Stigma? Changes in the Social Experience of Long-term Illness.* Abingdon: Routledge.

Hallowell, N. 1999: Doing the right thing: genetic risk and responsibility. *Sociology of Health and Illness,* 21, 597–621.

Hallowell, N., and Lawton, J. 2002: Negotiating present and future selves: managing the risk of hereditary ovarian cancer by prophylactic surgery. *Health,* 6, 423–43.

Hardey, M. 1999: Doctor in the house: the Internet as a source of lay health knowledge and the challenge to expertise. *Sociology of Health and Illness,* 21, 820–35.

Harley, D. 1999: Rhetoric and the social construction of sickness and healing. *Social History of Medicine,* 12, 408–35.

Heath, C., Luff, P., and Svensson, M. S. 2003: Technology and medical practice. *Sociology of Health and Illness,* 25, 75–96.

Helman, C. 1978: Feed a cold, starve a fever. *Culture Medicine and Psychiatry,* 2, 107–37.

Herzlich, C. 1973: *Health and Illness.* London: Academic Press.

Herzlich, C., and Pierret, J. 1985: The social construction of the patient: patients and illnesses in other ages. *Social Science and Medicine,* 20, 145–51.

—— 1987: *Illness and Self in Society.* Baltimore: Johns Hopkins University Press.

Heyman, J., Herzman, C. B., Currer, L. B., and Evans, R. G. (eds) 2006: *Healthier Societies: From Analysis to Action.* Oxford: Oxford University Press.

Hippocrates 1993: *Aphorisms,* trans. W. H. S. Jones. London and Cambridge, MA: Heinemann/Harvard University Press.

Hyden, L. C. 1997: Illness and narrative. *Sociology of Health and Illness,* 19, 48–69.

Illich, I. 1974: Medical nemesis. *The Lancet,* 11 May, 918–22.

Jewson, N. D. 1976: The disappearance of the sick man from medical cosmology 1770–1870. *Sociology,* 10, 225–44.

Jones, D. C., and Whitaker, M. I. 2009: *Speaking for the Dead.* Farnham: Ashgate.

Kelleher, D., and Leavey, G. (eds) 2004: *Identity and Health.* London: Routledge.

Kelly, J. 2008: *Magnetic Appeal: MRI and the Myth of Transparency*. New York: Cornell University Press.

Kendall, R. E. 1975: The concept of disease and its implications for psychiatry. *British Journal of Psychiatry*, 127, 305–15.

Kenen, R. 1994: The human genome project: creator of the potentially sick, potentially vulnerable and potentially stigmatized? In I. Robinson (ed.) *The Social Consequences of Life and Death under High Technology Medicine*. Manchester: Manchester University Press.

—— 1996: The at-risk health status and technology: a diagnostic invitation and the 'gift' of knowing. *Social Science and Medicine*, 42, 1545–53.

Kerr, A., and Shakespeare, T. 2002: *Genetic Politics. From Eugenics to Genome*. Cheltenham: New Clarendon Press.

Kleinman, A. 1980: *Patients and Healers in the Context of Culture: An Exploration of the Borderland between Anthropology, Medicine and Psychiatry*. Berkeley and London: University of California Press.

Koos, E. 1954: *The Health of Regionville: What the People Thought and Did About it*. New York: Columbia University Press.

Kunitz, S. J. 2001: Accounts of social capital: the mixed health effects of personal communities and voluntary groups. In D. Leon and G. Walt (eds) *Poverty, Inequality and Health*. Oxford: Oxford University Press, 159–74.

Kunst, A. E., Groenhof, F., Mackenbach, J. P., et al. 1998: Mortality by occupational class among men 30–64 years in 11 European countries. *Social Science and Medicine*, 46, 1459–76.

Lahelma, E., Kivela, K., Roos, E., et al. 2002: Analysing changes of health inequalities in the Nordic welfare states. *Social Science and Medicine*, 55, 609–25.

Lehoux, P. 2006: *The Problem of Health Technology: Policy Implications for Modern Health Care Systems*. Abingdon: Routledge.

Leon, D., and Walt, G. (eds) 2001: *Poverty, Inequality and Health*. Oxford: Oxford University Press.

Levy, N. 2007: *Neuroethics: Challenges for the 21st Century*. Cambridge: Cambridge University Press.

Linder, R. 1965: Diagnosis: description or prescription? A case study in the psychology of diagnosis. *Perceptual and Motor Skills*, 20, 1081–92.

Lock, M. 2002: *Twice Dead: Organ Transplants and the Reinvention of Death*. Berkeley and Los Angeles: University of California Press.

Lupton, D. 1995: *The Imperative of Health: Public Health and the Regulated Body*. London: Sage.

Macintyre, S. 1997: The Black Report and beyond: what are the issues? *Social Science and Medicine*, 44, 723–45.

McKee, M. 2001: The health consequences of the collapse of the Soviet Union. In D. Leon and G. Walt (eds) *Poverty, Inequality and Health*. Oxford: Oxford University Press, 17–36.

McKeown, T. 1976: *The Role of Medicine: Dream, Mirage or Nemesis?* London: Nuffield Provincial Hospitals Trust.

McKeown, T., Record, R. G., and Turner, R. D. 1975: An interpretation of the decline in mortality in England and Wales during the twentieth century. *Population Studies*, 29, 391–422.

Manning, N., and Tikhonova, N. (eds) 2009: *Health and Health Care in the New Russia*. Farnham: Ashgate.

Marmot, M. G. 2004: *Status Syndrome: How Your Social Standing Directly Affects Your Health and Life Expectancy*. London: Bloomsbury.

Marmot, M. G., and Feeney, A. 1996: Work and health: implications for individuals and society. In D. Blane, E. Brunner and R. Wilkinson (eds) *Health and Social Organisation*. London: Routledge.

Marmot, M. G., Shipley, M. J., and Rose, G. 1984: Inequalities in death-specific explanations of a general pattern. *The Lancet*, I, 1003–6.

Martin, E. 1987: *The Woman in the Body*. Milton Keynes: Open University Press.

—— 2000: Flexible bodies: science and a new culture of health in the US. In S. J. Williams, J. Gabe and M. Calnan (eds) *Health, Medicine and Society: Key Theories, Future Agendas*. London: Routledge, 123–45.

May, C., Gask, L., Atkinson, T., Ellis, N., and Mair, F. 2001: Resisting and promoting new technologies in clinical practice: the case of telepsychiatry. *Social Science and Medicine*, 52, 1889–901.

Mead, G. H. 1934: *Mind, Self and Society*. Chicago: University of Chicago Press.

Mechanic, D. 1968: *Medical Sociology*. New York: Free Press.

—— 2002: Socio-cultural implications of changing organizational technologies in the provision of care. *Social Science and Medicine*, 54, 459–67.

Michie, S., McDonald, V., and Marteau, T. 1996: Understanding responses to predictive genetic testing: a grounded theory approach. *Psychology and Health*, 11, 455–70.

Mishler, E. G. 1981: Critical perspectives on the biomedical model and the social construction of illness. In E. G. Mishler et al. (eds) *Social Contexts of Health, Illness and Patient Care.* Cambridge: Cambridge University Press.

Muntaner, C., Lynch, J., and Davey Smith, G. 2000: Social capital and the third way in public health. *Critical Public Health*, 10, 107–24.

Navarro, V. 1976: *Medicine under Capitalism.* London: Croom Helm.

—— (ed.) 2007: *Neoliberalism, Globalisation and Inequalities: Consequences for Health and Quality of Life.* Amityville, NY: Baywood.

Nelkin, D., and Andrews, L. 1999: DNA identification and surveillance creep. *Sociology of Health and Illness*, 21, 689–706.

Nettleton S., and Watson, J. (eds) 1998: *The Body in Everyday Life.* London: Routledge.

Neve, M. 1995: Ch. 8. In L. I. Conrad, M. Neve, V. Nutton, R. Porter and A. Wear (eds) *The Western Medical Tradition 800BC to AD1800.* Cambridge: Cambridge University Press, 477–94.

Nicolson, M., and McLaughlin, C. 1988: Social constructionism and medical sociology: a study of the vascular theory of multiple sclerosis. *Sociology of Health and Illness*, 10, 234–61.

Novas, C., and Rose, N. 2000: Genetic risk and the birth of the somatic individual. *Economy and Society*, 29, 485–513.

Oakley, A. 1976: Wisewomen and Medicineman: changes in the management of childbirth. In J. Mitchell and A. Oakley (eds) *The Rights and Wrongs of Women.* Harmondsworth: Penguin.

Parsons, T. 1951: *The Social System.* New York: Free Press.

Pasveer B. 1989: Knowledge of shadows: the introduction of X-rays in medicine. *Sociology of Health and Illness*, 11, 360–81.

Pierret, J. 1993: Constructing discourses about health and their social determinants. In A. Radley (ed.) *Worlds of Illness: Biographical and Cultural Perspectives on Health and Disease.* London: Routledge, 9–26.

Pill, R., and Stott, N. 1982: Concepts of illness causation and responsibility. *Social Science and Medicine*, 16, 43–52.

—— 1987: Development of a measure of potential health behaviour: a salience of lifestyle index. *Social Science and Medicine*, 24, 125–34.

Pollock, K. 1993: Attitude of mind as a means of resisting illness. In A. Radley (ed.) *Worlds of Illness: Biographical and Cultural Perspectives on Health and Disease.* London: Routledge, 49–70.

Porn, J. 1993: Health and adaptedness. *Theoretical Medicine*, 14, 295–303.

Posner, T. 1977: Magical elements in orthodox medicine: diabetes as a medical thought system. In R. Dingwall, C. Heath, M. Reid and M. Stacey (eds) *Health Care and Health Knowledge*. London: Croom Helm, 142–58.

Prior, L. 2000: Reflection on the 'mortal' body in late modernity. In S. J. Williams, J. Gabe and M. Calnan (eds) *Health, Medicine and Society: Key Theories, Future Agendas*. London: Routledge, 186–202.

—— 2003: Belief, knowledge and expertise: the emergence of the lay expert in medical sociology. *Sociology of Health and Illness*, 25, 41–57.

Prior, L., Wood, F., Gray, J., Pill, R., and Hughes, D. 2002: Making risk visible: the role of images in the assessment of (cancer) genetic risk. *Health Risk and Society*, 4, 241–58.

Putnam, R. D. 1995: Bowling alone: America's declining social capital. *Journal of Democracy*, 6, 65–78.

Quah, S. 2001: Health and culture. In W. C. Cockerham (ed.) *The Blackwell Companion to Medical Sociology*. Oxford: Blackwell, 23–42.

Radley, A., and Billig, M. 1996: Accounts of health and illness: dilemmas and representations. *Sociology of Health and Illness*, 18, 220–40.

Radley, A., and Green, R. 1987: Illness and adjustment. *Sociology of Health and Illness*, 9, 179–207.

Robinson, D. 1971: *The Process of Becoming Ill*. London: Routledge and Kegan Paul.

Rosenstock, I. M. 1974: Historical origins of the health belief model. *Health Education Monographs*, 2, 328–35.

Sanner, M. A. 2001: Exchanging spare parts or becoming a new person? People's attitudes toward receiving and donating organs. *Social Science and Medicine*, 52, 1491–9.

Scheff, T. J. 1966: *Being Mentally Ill: A Sociological Theory*. Chicago: Aldine.

Scott, R. A. 1966: The selection of clients by social welfare agencies: the case of the blind. *Social Problems*, 14.

Scott, W. J. 1990: PTSD in DSM-III: a case in the politics of diagnosis and disease. *Social Problems*, 37, 294–310.

Seale, C. 2000: Changing patterns of death and dying. *Social Science and Medicine*, 51, 917–30.

Seale, C., and Pattison, S. (eds) 1994: *Medical Knowledge: Doubt and Certainty*. Buckingham: Open University Press.

Sedgwick, P. 1973: Illness, mental and otherwise. *Hastings Center Studies*, 1, 19–40.

Sharp, L. A. 1995: Organ transplantations as a transformative experience: anthropological insights into the restructuring of the self. *Medical Anthropology Quarterly*, 9, 357–89.

Shilling, C. 1993: *The Body and Social Theory*. London: Sage.

Sontag, S. 1979: *Illness as Metaphor*. New York: Vintage.

Stainton Rogers, W. 1991: *Explaining Health and Illness*. London: Harvester Wheatsheaf.

Swann, C., and Morgan, A. (eds) 2002: *Social Capital for Health: Insights from Qualitative Research*. London: Health Development Agency.

Szasz, T. S. 1961: *The Myth of Mental Illness*. London: Secker and Warburg.

Tarlov, A. R. 1996: Social determinants of health: the sociobiological translation. In D. Blane, E. Brunner and R. Wilkinson (eds) *Health and Social Organisation*. London: Routledge.

Timmermans, S., and Berg, M. 2003: The practice of medical technology. *Sociology of Health and Illness*, 25 97–114.

Turner B. S. 1984: *The Body and Society*. London: Sage.

—— 1996: *Regulating Bodies*. London: Routledge.

Wadsworth, M. E. J. 1991: *The Imprint of Time*. Oxford: Clarendon Press.

Waldby, C. 1998: Medical imaging: the biopolitics of visibility. *Health*, 2, 372–84.

—— 2002: Stem cells, tissue cultures and the production of biovalue. *Health*, 6, 305–23.

Wear, A. (ed.) 1992: *Medicine in Society: Historical Essays*. Cambridge: Cambridge University Press.

Webster, A. 2007: *Health Technology and Society, a Sociological Critique*. Basingstoke: Palgrave Macmillan.

Wertz, D. C. 1992: Ethical and legal implications of the new genetics. *Social Science and Medicine*, 35, 495–505.

Wilkinson, R. 1996: *Unhealthy Societies: The Afflictions of Inequality*. London: Routledge.

—— 2000: *Mind the Gap: Hierarchies, Health and Human Evolution*. London: Weidenfeld and Nicolson.

Williams, G. 1993: Chronic illness and the pursuit of virtue in everyday life. In A. Radley (ed.) *Worlds of Illness: Biographical and Cultural Perspectives on Health and Disease*. London: Routledge, 92–108.

Williams, G., and Busby, H. 2000: The politics of 'disabled' bodies. In S. J. Williams, J. Gabe and M. Calnan (eds) *Health, Medicine and Society: Key Theories, Future Agendas*. London: Routledge, 169–85.

Williams, R. 1990: *A Protestant Legacy*. Oxford: Clarendon Press.

Williams, S. J. 1996: The vicissitudes of embodiment across the chronic illness trajectory. *Body and Society*, 2, 23–47.

—— 1997: Modern medicine and the 'uncertain body': from corporeality to hyperreality? *Social Science and Medicine*, 45, 1041–9.

Williams, S. J., and Bendelow, G. 1998: *The Lived Body: Sociological Themes, Embodied Issue*s. London: Routledge.

Williams S. J., Birke, L., and Bendelow, G. 2003: *Debating Biology: Sociological Relections on Health, Medicine and Society*. London: Routledge.

Williams, S. J., Gabe, J., and Calnan, M. (eds) 2000: *Health Medicine and Society: Key Theories, Future Agendas*. London: Routledge.

World Health Organization, Regional Office for Europe, 1998: *Health 21: Health for All in the 21st Century*. Copenhagen: WHO.

Wyatt, J. C. 1996: Commentary: telemedicine trials – clinical pull or technology push? *MB Journal*, 313, 1380–1.

Zola, I. K. 1973: Pathways to the doctor – from person to patient. *Social Science and Medicine*, 7, 677–89.

—— 1975: Medicine as an institution of social control. In C. Cox and A. Mead (eds) *A Sociology of Medical Practice*. New York: Macmillan.

Index